# UNUSUAL BIBLE
# INTERPRETATIONS

# JUDGES

# Israel Drazin

gefen
publishing house
JERUSALEM ◆ NEW YORK   Est. 1981

Cover design: Leah Ben Avraham/ Noonim Graphics
Typesetting: Renana Typesetting

ISBN: 978-965-229-710-5

1 3 5 7 9 8 6 4 2

Gefen Publishing House Ltd.
6 Hatzvi Street
Jerusalem 94386, Israel
972-2-538-0247
orders@gefenpublishing.com

Gefen Books
11 Edison Place
Springfield, NJ 07081
516-593-1234
orders@gefenpublishing.com

**www.gefenpublishing.com**

Printed in Israel                    *Send for our free catalog*

Library of Congress Cataloging-in-Publication Data

Drazin, Israel, 1935– author.
  Unusual Bible interpretations : Judges / by Israel Drazin.
      pages cm
  Includes bibliographical references and index.
  ISBN 978-965-229-710-5
  1.  Bible. Judges--Criticism, interpretation, etc.  I. Title.
  BS1305.52.D73 2015
  222'.3206--dc23

2015025414

*Dedicated to Dina*

# Contents

# Acknowledgments

I want to thank Darlene Jospe who has been performing the first editing of all my books since I began to write *Onkelos on the Torah* with Stanley Wagner. She also helped mightily with formatting and preparing indexes.

I also want to thank Dr. Jack Cohen who studies Torah with me every Wednesday morning from ten to eleven. I write these essays as my contribution to our study.

I also give thanks to Tziporah Levine, my excellent editor, and to Gefen Publishing House, which has published many of my books and has agreed to publish the series of books I call Unusual Bible Interpretations.

# Introduction

*The twenty-one chapters of the biblical book Judges introduces readers to the life of the Israelite tribes after the death of Joshua. While the tribes were united under Moses and Joshua, they became disconnected following Joshua's death and waged wars to conquer land in Canaan as single tribes, although they sometimes joined with other tribes.[1] The book gives no reason for the breakup from a unified nation to self-interested tribes.[2]*

### WHEN WAS THE BOOK AUTHORED AND BY WHOM?

According to a talmudic view,[3] Samuel wrote the book named after him as well as the books of Judges and Ruth. Others[4] insist that Judges was composed during the reign of King David, or King Solomon, or King Josiah,[5] or even as late as the

---

1. The unified nation of Israel appears in this book in only three instances: the critique of the "angel" in 2:4, Gideon's *ephod* in 8:27, and the outrage at the city Gibeah in 20:1. However these references to "all of Israel" may be hyperbolic and mean "many Israelites," not every tribe.

2. This has led many scholars, such as Arnold Ehrlich, to believe that (1) Joshua was a mythological figure, (2) the Israelites began as tribes and only later unified as a nation, (3) the author of Judges knew nothing about Joshua, and (4) the initial parts of Judges that mention a leader called Joshua were added by an editor who wanted to connect the two books.

Ehrlich supports his view that the author of Judges knew nothing about Joshua – the man or the book – by detailing the many differences between the two books, such as the book Joshua stating that Joshua conquered certain cities while Judges describes them as being vanquished only after Joshua's death, and not by all of Israel, but only by isolated tribes. Similarly, verse 10 states that Kenites traveled from "the city of palm trees" to Judah's territory; the "city of palm trees" is generally understood as Jericho, and is so identified in the Aramaic translation Targum Jonathan. But according to Joshua 6, Joshua utterly destroyed Jericho; thus Judges is in conflict with Joshua.

3. Babylonian Talmud, *Bava Batra* 14b.

4. Such as *Olam Hatanakh*, ed. Menachem Haran (Jerusalem / Tel Aviv: Davidson-Atai, 1995, Hebrew).

5. 641–609 BCE. King Josiah instituted a reformation of Judaism. This story is found in II Kings 22–23 and II Chronicles 34–35.

Judean exile in 586 BCE, perhaps no earlier than 550 BCE.[6] Yehezkel Kaufmann suggests that the book was edited some five hundred to six hundred years after the events it narrates, but some of the material in it dates back to an earlier time.

## THE CYCLIC NATURE OF JUDGES

While the book of Joshua portrays the Israelites loyally accepting the divine covenant offered to them by Joshua, Judges states the Israelites repeatedly did "what was evil in the sight of God."[7] They committed two wrongs: they abandoned God's covenant when they worshipped idols, and they allowed the Canaanites to remain in their territory.[8] The author writes that the same events were repeated, often in a cyclic pattern. After acting improperly, Israel is punished by an adversary;[9] the people pray to God for help[10] and a "judge" (a term I will explain below) appears and in a military manner saves the people; the land then remains "calm" for a designated period. These series of cyclic stories usually end with a mention of the hero's death.[11]

## WHAT IS A "JUDGE"?

The book mentions fourteen of fifteen or seventeen judges,[12] who came from many different walks of life, including one woman – Deborah. Two of the judges, Eli and Samuel, are not in the book Judges but in 1 Samuel. Some of the judges have extensive descriptions of their exploits, but little information is given about five judges. For want of a better title, some scholars call these five "minor judges."[13] There is no indication that the minor judges led Israelites in war, as did the major ones.

---

6. The argument is made that the book of Judges shows that the Israelites are punished for their misdeeds, and the book was composed after the exile from Judea to explain why many Judeans were exiled from their country.

7. 3:7, 12; 4:1; 6:1; 10:6; and 13:1.

8. This is the view of Kaufmann.

9. 3:8, 12; 4:2; 6:16; 10:7; 13:1.

10. Judges describes a nation whose people attributed everything, good and bad, to God.

11. 3:11, 30; 5:31; 8:28–32; 12:7; 15:20; 16:31.

12. There were only fourteen judges if Shamgar was a non-Israelite, as discussed in chapter 3, and only thirteen if we delete Samson. The exact number of Judges is discussed in chapter 10.

13. They appear in 10:1–5 and 12:8–15. The length of service of the major judges is given in round stereotypical numbers (20, 40, 80 – the sole exception is Jephthah in 12:7, whose service was

The book contains twenty-one chapters. The tale of the last judge, Samson, is recorded in chapters 13–16, and some scholars feel that the Samson saga as well as what follows it were not part of the original book of Judges. However, other scholars accept the entire book as the original version because, among other reasons, the remaining part of the book creates a chiastic structure with the beginning of the book: both parts portray the improper acts of individual tribes.

While the English translation of the Hebrew *shophtim* is "judges,"[14] scholars understand the term to denote a governmental and leadership function, not just a judicial one.[15] Some scholars call these *shophtim* "charismatic leaders."[16] The Aramaic translation Targum Jonathan translates *shophtim* in 2:16 as *negidin*, "leaders." II Kings 15:5 calls King Azariah's son a "judge." He took over the reign of his father when his father was secluded because he was inflicted with leprosy. Ehrlich comments: "This shows that that the Bible calls a ruler who is not a king a *shophet*."

HOW LONG DID THE JUDGES JUDGE?

No one knows how long the period of the judges lasted and there are many speculations about it. The author of I Kings 6:1 states that King Solomon began to construct the temple in Jerusalem in the fourth year of his reign, which was "the 480th year" after the exodus from Egyptian slavery.[17] If this figure is taken literally, and the reigns of Kings Saul and David and the four years of Solomon's kingship are deducted, the judges would have functioned for about four hundred years.[18] Recently, some scholars claimed that they found items that support the contention that the Hebrews entered Egypt around 1700 BCE, the exodus occurred

---

for 6 years), but those of the minor judges are given in precise numbers (23, 22, 10, 7, 8). It is possible that since the Jephthah narrative is told in the midst of the brief tales of the minor judges, this influenced mentioning a precise number.

14. This is also how the ancient Aramaic translation Targum Jonathan translates it.

15. In the book of Judges, the word is used as a noun only in 2:16–18 to describe the heroes and in 11:27 where Jephthah portrays God as a *shophet*. It is also used in II Samuel 7:11, II Kings 23:22, Ruth 1:1, and I Chronicles 17:6, 10.

16. J.D. Martin, *The Book of Judges*, Cambridge Bible Commentary Series (London: Cambridge University, 1962).

17. In Judges 11:26, Jephthah states that the Israelites dwelt in Heshbon for 300 years. At first blush this would seem to support the figure of 480, for the long period of 480 would include the years after Jephthah until King Solomon. However, scholars understand Jephthah to be speaking about the time since Moses conquered the city.

18. The exodus from Egyptian bondage according to this account would be around 1440 BCE.

about 1500 BCE, and the period of the judges lasted about four hundred years. The artifacts included pictures of people dressed as Hebrews, the name Yaakov, and early Hebrew writing.[19]

However, other scholars[20] suggest that 480 is another of the many stereotypical instances where Scripture states that a leader led the Israelites for forty years.[21] They suggest that the biblical author felt that forty meant a generation and that twelve generations passed from the exodus to the time of King Solomon. If, the scholars say, one would substitute 20–25 as the figure for a generation, the time would be about 240 years, which is the number that some scholars assign to the period of the judges. John Bright's view, which is accepted by many scholars, is that the exodus occurred around 1200 BCE and King Saul reigned as king around 1020 BCE;[22] thus the period of the judges was only about 200 years.[23]

WHERE DOES THE BOOK BEGIN AND END?

Most critical scholars are convinced that a beginning and ending were added to the original book of Judges which was not part of the original text, but they differ regarding the details. George Foot Moore[24] recognizes that some scholars end the first introduction at 2:5, and writes: "That 2:1–5 is to be joined to [chapter] 1 is now generally recognized; 2:1–5 is the fitting close of the account of the conquest and settlement in chapter 1." Moore feels that 2:6 through 3:6 is a second introduction; it tells how the Israelite tribes began to abandon God soon after the death of Joshua and the elders of his generation, how God punished them by having them suffer at the hands of Canaanites, and how judges saved them.

Some scholars contend that the book of Judges itself begins with 3:7 and ends with 13:1 just before the tales of Samson, for they feel that the stories of Samson and the other tales now concluding Judges were added by an editor after the book

---

19. This is discussed in the 2006 film *The Exodus Decoded* by Simcha Jacobovici.
20. Such as John Bright in *A History of Israel*, 2nd ed. (London: SCM Press, 1972). See below.
21. Such as Moses, David, and several judges in this book.
22. Solomon ascended the throne, according to Bright, around 961 BCE.
23. If one used the "anno mundi" calendar, the generally faulty calculation of time since the creation of the world, one would come out with approximately the same figure. The year that I am writing this book is 5775 (2015), the exodus was in 2448, or 3327 years ago, which is 1312 BCE. Add forty years of desert wondering until the entry into Canaan and fourteen years of Joshua's leadership and that brings one to the onset of the period of the judges after 1258 BCE.
24. *Judges*, International Critical Commentary, 2nd rev. ed. (T. and T. Clark, 2000).

was completed. The Interpreter's Bible[25] includes the Samson story in the original book of Judges and contends that the book ended in 16:31. Yehuda Elitzur[26] divides Judges into three parts: the introductions until 2:6, the body of the work until 16:31, and part three being the conclusion.

25. Abingdon Press, 1953.
26. In *Sefer Shophtim*, Daat Mikra (Jerusalem: Mossad Harav Kook, 1976).

# PART ONE

# CHAPTERS 1–2

# BETWEEN JOSHUA AND THE JUDGES

*The introductory chapters of Judges bridge the period from Joshua to the judges. While the book of Joshua states that the Israelites were united during the leadership of Joshua, and were loyal to God, they ceased being so after he died.*

# Chapter 1

# *Judah Is First*

*The first chapter of Judges seems to describe actions by Israelite tribes after Joshua's death and before the appearance of the first judge.[1] Instead of a named leader leading the tribe or united nation in war, each tribe functioned in its own self-interest. The tribes battled the Canaanites to take their land. Judges appeared after the tribes settled in tribal territories, when they ignored the will of God, were attacked by enemy forces, and required a savior. Chapter 1 describes the successes of the tribe of Judah as well as the failures of the other tribes.*

A BRIEF SUMMARY

After Joshua died, the Israelites inquired of God which tribe should attack the Canaanites first. "The Lord answered, 'Judah shall attack. I will deliver the country into his power.'" The tribe of Simeon joined Judah; together they successfully fought many battles.

Caleb, a leader of the tribe of Judah, offers his daughter Achsah to whomever captures Kiriath-sepher, and his nephew Othniel does so in a story repeated from the book of Joshua. The descendants of Moses's father-in-law, the Kenites, left the city of palms and settled in the Judean territory. Although usually successful, Judah was unable to drive out the inhabitants of the city of palms "because they had chariots of iron."

---

1. However, while the chapter speaks about the tribe of Judah taking the initiative in fighting for land and mentions no leader, Rashi states that "there are those who state [that the words] 'Judah shall go' refers to [the first judge] Othniel." Similarly, Rashi comments that the tribes wanted to know which would be the first tribe that would attempt to secure the land that Joshua had assigned to each tribe – even though the chapter gives no indication that the land in question had been allotted by Joshua.

In contrast to Judah's triumphs, the tribe of Benjamin failed to conquer Jerusalem and other tribes were generally unsuccessful as well. The tribes of Joseph took Beth-el, but only by promising not to harm its inhabitants – a promise they were quick to break as "they put the city to the sword."

QUESTIONS

This chapter raises many questions, such as:

1. What is the purpose of this chapter, which repeats much of what was revealed in the book of Joshua?
2. Did the recorded events occur before or after Joshua's death?
3. Why was the tribe of Judah generally effective while the other tribes usually failed?
4. Did Judah have a military or political leader at that time?
5. Given that God promised that Israel would conquer Canaan, why didn't God help Israel?[2] Why did the tribes of Joseph need to lie to gain success?
6. Should we understand the story in a natural way – that God does not manipulate the laws of nature and help people, but expects people to work out their own destiny?
7. Alternatively, if we accept the view that God helps people, what did Israel do to stop the divine aid during the conquest?
8. The rabbis in the Midrash offer pious, supernatural explanations of the events mentioned in this chapter. Should we understand these statements literally or read their comments as parables designed to provoke thinking?
9. Should we believe that biblical numbers are precise?
10. Are there mistakes in this biblical book?

JUDAH VS. JOSEPH

One possible purpose of Judges is that the author or authors wanted to extol the

---

2. Many people understood biblical prophecies as predictions of what will occur, such as the prophecy regarding the successful conquest of Canaan. However others, such as Tosaphot on *Yevamot* 50a (s.v. *teida*) and Malbim on Isaiah 11, saw prophecies as predictions of what *should* happen. In fact, they note that most if not all famous biblical prophecies never transpired.

tribe of Judah. During the early reign of King Solomon's son Rehoboam, around 922 BCE, ten tribes disassociated themselves from the tribe of Judah and formed the northern kingdom of Israel. The kingdom lasted for about two hundred years until 722 BCE, when it was conquered and the inhabitants exiled. They are called the "ten lost tribes" because we have no idea what happened to them.[3] Judah in the south lasted until 586 BCE, when the kingdom was defeated by the Babylonians and many Judeans were exiled to Babylon.

Some scholars maintain that the author(s) of Judges is showing that Judah is far superior to Joseph, the tribe that assumed leadership in the northern country of Israel. Thus Judah is shown assuming the leadership role at the outset of the period of the judges: when the tribes asked which of them was willing to be the first to attempt to conquer and hold Canaanite land Judah agreed to do so, while the other tribes sat back hesitantly, perhaps in fear, waiting to measure Judah's success. Judah also demonstrates leadership at the conclusion of Judges in 20:18, where God states that Judah should lead the people in battle. Chapter one describes Judah being repeatedly successful not only in defeating Canaanites in their own territory but even Canaanites dwelling far to the north, south, and west, in valiant and intrepid battles.

In contrast, the tribe of Ephraim, part of Joseph, is portrayed as attempting to assume leadership twice, in 8:1–3 and 12:1–6, and failing. The tribes of Joseph succeeded in defeating a single city, not by power but by using stealth and deception, by finding a way to enter the city without its inhabitants knowing that they were being attacked. The tribe of Dan, one of the future parts of the kingdom of Israel, was totally unable to vanquish the Canaanites and take land it desired. The tribe had to settle in the far north, obtaining land only by beating a peaceful nation.

PIOUS EXPLANATIONS

After a series of successes, Judah was unable "to drive out the inhabitants of the valley because they had chariots of iron."[4] This scriptural explanation accords

---

3. They apparently assimilated.

4. As with other books of the Prophets, and as we saw in my discussions of Joshua, the book has many errors. One is in this verse (19). The word "able" is missing, apparently a scribal oversight. The Greek translation, the Septuagint, adds the word, as does the Aramaic translation Targum Jonathan.

with what we know of the time: this was the beginning of the Iron Age and Israel had not yet developed the capability of using iron, as we will also see in future chapters. However, commentators such as Rashi, Radak, and Gersonides were bothered by the question: Wasn't God helping the tribes and doesn't God have the power to overcome iron chariots? They answer that God didn't help Judah at this time because the tribe had acted improperly.[5] They also use this excuse to explain the failures of the other tribes.

These commentators give another reason why God didn't help Benjamin capture Jerusalem: Abraham had made a covenant with Abimelech in Genesis 21:23–27 that his descendants would not harm Abimelech's descendants until the time of his great grandchildren, and Abimelech's great grandchildren were still alive at that time.[6]

Why did the Kenites travel from Jericho to the Judah territory? Rashi explains that they went to learn Torah from Othniel, the first judge.

## STEREOTYPICAL NUMBERS

The Bible is filled with stereotypical round numbers that should not be taken literally, and this book is no exception. A few examples will suffice: (1) Judah slaughters ten thousand[7] enemy forces in 1:4; (2) After being captured, the Canaanite king Adoni-bezek[8] told the tribe of Judah that he was repaid for what he had done – as he had subjugated seventy Canaanite kings;[9] (3) Several judges are reported to have served for forty years.[10]

---

5. There is no mention in the chapter of any wrong committed by an individual or by the entire tribe of Judah.

6. Abimelech was a Philistine. These commentators thus assume that the Philistines, who dwelt on the Mediterranean coast, were occupying Jerusalem at that time.

7. Some scholars say the Hebrew *eleph* should not be translated "thousand," but military units. Thus Judah vanquished ten military units. It is used in 6:15 in this way.

8. Why did Judah cut off Adoni-bezek's thumb and big toe? Judges gives no reason. Various ideas have been offered, such as: to make it impossible for him to fight if he escapes; to deter other Canaanites from fighting, given the frightening consequence; and to disqualify Adoni-bezek from the priesthood, assuming he was a priest.

9. The number seventy also appears, among other places, in Exodus 24; Numbers 11; Judges 9:2, 5; and Judges 12:14. See my *Maimonides and the Biblical Prophets* (Jerusalem: Gefen Publishing House, 2009), chapter 39, for a discussion of the significance of numbers in the Bible.

10. And in 13:1 the Philistines lorded over Israel for forty years.

# Chapter 2

# *The Tribes Abandon God*

---

*Chapter 2 continues what most critical scholars feel is an introduction appended to the original book of Judges. While a superficial reading of the chapter may disclose no problems, an open-minded reading reveals many problems.*

---

## AN ANGEL APPEARS AND CRITIQUES THE PEOPLE

Chapter 2 states that an angel appeared to the entire Israelite community and criticized them for failing to obey God's command to drive out the Canaanites from Canaan.[1] This critique is strange and seemingly inappropriate because we just read that the people didn't abandon God during the lifetime of Joshua and the elders[2] who led the people after him, so there is no ground for criticism. Therefore,

---

1. An angel also appears to Gideon and to Samson's mother in chapters 6:11 and 13:3, respectively. Moore contends that "angel" is a reference to God; this was a divine prophecy. He adds that the theophany at Beth-el is a sign from God that a sanctuary with an altar can be built there, along with the one at Shiloh. The idea that the angel appeared at Beth-el is based on the Septuagint translation that adds this name. See below, under "More Errors." The Aramaic translation Targum Jonathan, Robert G. Boling, and others identify the angel as an unnamed prophet. Rashi, Radak, *Midrash Leviticus Rabba* 1:1, *Midrash Numbers Rabba* 16:1, *Midrash Tanchuma Shelach* 1, and *Seder Olam*, among others, suppose the "angel" was the priest Pinchas, grandson of Moses's brother Aaron.

The Pentateuch ban on making peace with the Canaanites is in Exodus 22:32–33, 34:15, and Deuteronomy 7:2. Moses changes the mandate in Deuteronomy 20:10 and required the Israelites to petition for peace before a battle.

2. While Joshua 24:31 states the Israelites did not abandon God during the lifetime of the elders, it most likely means most of the elders (Gersonides and Abarbanel). As I pointed out frequently, the Bible writes hyperbolically; "all" means many. The length of the period of Joshua and the elders is unknown. In his commentary to the Babylonian Talmud, *Shabbat* 105b, Rashi states it was twenty-six years.

some critical scholars such as Ehrlich argue that the episode of the appearance of the angel (2:1–5) is misplaced. It belongs somewhere after the beginning of the period of the judges, who emerged because the Israelites abandoned God.

MORE ERRORS

Verse 1 has a space in the middle of the verse: "And the angel of the Lord came up from Gilgal to Bochim. [    ] And he said, 'I made you go up out of Egypt.'" Scholars suggest that the space indicates the feeling of an editor or scribe that something is missing. The Septuagint translation adds "and to Beth-el and to the house of Israel."

There is an error in verse 3, again missing words. It reads: "I also said, I will not drive them out from before you." The Septuagint translation makes the verse clearer: "I will no longer drive out the people whom I had said I would dispossess."[3] While "I also said" is in the past tense and seems to imply that God made the decision not to drive out the Canaanites before the Israelites acted improperly, this is not an error. Scripture very frequently uses the future for the past tense and vice versa.[4] The verse should be understood as "I have now decided."[5]

Verse 9 states that Joshua was buried in Timnath-heres but in Joshua 19:50 and 24:30 the place is referred to as Timnath-serah.

Verse 15 appears to miss the word "place," which the Aramaic translation Targum Jonathan adds. Judges reads: "In every…that they go out, the hand of God will be against them for evil." Rashi[6] states that this punishment refers to Elimelech and his two sons for abandoning the land of Judea during a period of draught in Ruth 1. Radak calls this imaginative *derash*.

REPETITIONS THAT CONFLICT

The chapter is filled with repetitions, some of which seem to conflict with other statements. This led some scholars, such as Moore in the International Critical

---

3. Numbers 33:50–56 states that if the Israelites do not drive out the Canaanites they will harass the Israelites.
4. Scripture also uses the plural for the singular and vice versa many times.
5. Abarbanel explains that the verse should be understood as depicting a present decision, as I wrote, but he does not discuss the biblical style here.
6. Relying on *Seder Olam*.

Commentary, to suppose that there is a conflation of two divergent traditions.[7] The editor of Judges found the two and combined them without bothering to harmonize them. In one, called D, "the sin of Israel is the worship of the Baals and Astartes."[8] In the other, called E, it is "the adoption of the religion of the surrounding nations." In E they are delivered into the hand of plunderers; in D they are sold into the power of the enemies who surround them. In E they do not obey their judges but persist in apostasy even during the reign of the judges. In D, the Israelites do not abandon God during the lifetime of the judge who saves them.

E states that God determined that the conquest would be incomplete because of the people's apostasy. Yet in 3:2, attributed to D, there is an altogether different explanation for the incompleteness of the conquest: God let some Canaanite nations remain in the land "to teach them [the Israelites] war, at least such as beforetime knew nothing thereof."

In 2:21, a third reason for God's failure to drive out the Canaanites is given: to test Israel to see whether they "keep the way of the Lord."

A fourth, totally different reason is found in Exodus 23:29 and Deuteronomy 7:22: God will not drive the nations out "in one year, lest the land become desolate and the beasts of the field multiply against you."

Critical commentators insist that these divergences show that there were different authors who offered their own opinions or retold a diverse tradition, and the editor assembled them without harmonizing them.

## AN INSULTING CRITIQUE OF JUDGES'S PORTRAYAL OF GOD AND ISRAEL

The author of the Interpreter's Bible offers a scathing condemnation of ancient Israel.[9] He writes that in Judges as well as in the book of Joshua, "any compassion,

---

7. An example of conflation in the Pentateuch is the story of the sale of Joseph. The only way one can understand the story of the kidnapping of Joseph and his sale into slavery (37:18–30) is that it is a conflation of two versions. In one, Reuben is the brother who tries to save Joseph. In the second, it is Judah. In one, the brothers take Joseph from the pit and sell him to Ishmaelites. In the other, Midianites lifted Joseph from the pit and sold him to Ishmaelites.

8. Baal means lord, proprietor, and possessor. It is not a name. There were many different Baals worshipped by the nations in the area. The most famous Baal was a storm god. The Asherah is also mentioned in 3:7. It is called Astarte in 10:6; the editor did not attempt to harmonize the texts. This feminine deity was the god of fertility. The biblical Esther was named after Astarte, and Mordechai after the god Marduk.

9. We will see his similar attack on the judge Ehud in chapter 3.

any redemptive overture toward the Canaanites is undreamed of. We are far from a concept of God as the Father of all men; he is here the tribal deity, intent upon establishing his own people and determining to defeat their and his enemies." This author also berates the Israelites: "God has not broken his promise, but Israel has broken hers." Israel gives no answer "except the answer of tears."

The censure of the Interpreter's Bible is overstated. Any evaluation of the moral nature of the Bible must examine the Bible in its totality, not only a single event or a single command. The author of the Interpreter's Bible forgot that the Bible is filled with teachings that people must treat others, even animals, with respect. For example, it repeats the command "Love the stranger," meaning non-Israelites, thirty-six times. There are several commands that show the Bible's sensitivity not only to humans, but also to animals, such as Numbers 20:7 where God instructs Moses to hit a rock and cause it to flow water for both people and animals.

According to the Bible, the tribes knew that the land of Canaan was theirs and the Canaanites were appropriating land that did not belong to them. Moses told them in the Pentateuch that before attempting to retake the land they should sue for peace. Deuteronomy 20:10 states: "When you approach a city to wage war against it, you must propose a peaceful settlement." Maimonides writes[10] that the Israelites were not only allowed to make peace with the Canaanites, they were obligated to do so if at all reasonable. So, contrary to the Interpreter's Bible, while many Israelites during the period of the judges had not yet matured, the Bible did teach compassion.

Maimonides built a remarkable philosophy upon the event mentioned in Exodus 13:17. The Torah states there that instead of taking the Israelites on a direct trip to Canaan, God led the Israelites on a roundabout route so that they would not have to fight the Philistines. God knew that when they would be attacked by the Philistines, these erstwhile slaves would become fearful and rush back to their former Egyptian masters.

Maimonides stressed[11] that the Torah recognized that it is "impossible to go suddenly from one extreme to another; it is . . . impossible for him to suddenly

---

10. In his *Mishneh Torah, Hilkhot Melakhim*, chapters 5 and 6. See also the Jerusalem Talmud, *Sheviit* 6:1.
11. In his *Guide of the Perplexed* 3:32.

discontinue everything to which he has been accustomed." Thus the Torah had to deal with the then-existing primitive mindset of the people.

The Torah did so, for example, with sacrifices. Maimonides was opposed to sacrifices. He felt that "it is for this reason God *allowed* these kinds of service to continue" – not because it is good for people to offer sacrifices or that God needs sacrifices, but because the people had become so accustomed to it and saw other nations offering sacrifices. However, as Maimonides goes on to explain, the Torah limited sacrifices dramatically: where they could be brought, when, how, and which type of animals. The Torah allowed sacrifices in a way that encouraged the people to realize it was wrong.

According to Maimonides, many commands in the Torah were only instituted because of the weakness of human nature and were meant to cease as people improved. The principle applies to the laws of slavery, witchcraft, the evil son, the captive woman, and an eye for an eye, among others. Each of these laws is contrary to basic morality. The Torah allowed the Israelites to have slaves, kill suspected witches, and execute evil sons; it permitted a soldier to have sex and marry women captured during wars; and it retained the ancient retaliatory notion of an eye for an eye – but all of these customs were permitted only under the most restrictive procedures.[12] And the Torah is written in a way that encourages people to act in a better manner than what is *allowed.*

The mindset of non-Israelites at the time of Joshua and the judges was conquest, total extinction of the inhabitants, rape, and enslavement. The Torah had to deal with this worldview. The early parts of the Pentateuch accepted the notion of total extinction, but later Moses changed the command to obligate seeking peace. The Israelites during the period of the judges went further and allowed the Canaanites to remain in land the Canaanites felt was theirs.[13]

It is possible to read the angel's critique (2:1–3) as, "OK, you permitted the Canaanites to remain, but you did so in a foolish manner. You allowed them to seduce you to worship their idols."

---

12. Countless Orthodox Jews reject Maimonides's understanding of the purpose of these commands, and think that every Torah command is proper, moral, and ideal.

13. This idea – that the Israelites were willing to abandon the feeling that they must exile all non-Israelites from their land and their moral willingness to let these people remain where they had lived for some years – is not explicit in Judges.

Relationships between the Israelites and pagans improved to the extent that two non-Israelites, Shamgar[14] and Yael, aided the Israelites by killing Israelite enemies, as indicated in Judges 3 and 4.

Thus the Interpreter's Bible censure is unfair. The Torah allowed certain ancient practices but encouraged the people to act in a better manner. The story of the conquest shows a development of a humane treatment of enemy forces – not yet ideal, but moving in the proper direction. Even in this ancient time, the Israelites behaved more humanely than other nations.[15]

---

14. Many scholars are convinced that Shamgar was a non-Israelite. See chapter 3.

15. Ancient Athens, for example, is considered by many scholars to be the cradle of philosophy and morality. It is the birthplace of Socrates, Plato, and Aristotle. Yet Rebecca Newberger Goldstein portrays fifth-century Athens engaging in horrendous, murderous, unjust acts during war in her *Plato at the Googleplex: Why Philosophy Won't Go Away* (Pantheon, 2014), pages 298–300.

**Excursus**

# Should People Believe in Angels?

*The Bible mentions angels in chapter 2. Should we interpret this allusion symbolically, and deny the existence of angels, or understand the passages literally, and insist that not only do angels exist but that they are involved in and impact upon our lives?*

## JACOB AND ANGELS

In Genesis 28:12 one can find one of many instances of biblical references to angels. Jacob abandoned his family home in fear of his brother Esau's revenge after Jacob took the blessing their father Isaac had intended for Esau. Jacob has a dream on the first night away from home which expresses his fear. He sees a ladder reaching up to heaven with angels ascending and descending its steps.

A rationalist would understand that the Bible is describing a dream depicting Jacob's fears and the angels are symbolic figures that assuage Jacob's distress and give him a sense of security. The nonrationalist sees the dream as biblical confirmation of the existence of angels who will protect Jacob.

## VARIOUS VIEWS ABOUT ANGELS

The term *malakh*, which is frequently translated as "angel," literally means "messenger." The term can be understood as a metaphor for the forces of nature. On the other hand, people can see in this term a description of a supernatural being that is superior to humans in power and knowledge, but not as powerful as God. People who understand the term *malakh* in this way may also believe in the existence of incorporeal life forms that perform evil acts, frequently contrary to God's will. They may name them demons or evil angels.

## MAIMONIDES

Moses Maimonides (1138–1204) and Moses Nachmanides (1195–1270) express polar-opposite conceptions of angels, and there are many other intermediate ideas held by other people. Maimonides rejected the notion that angels are divine-like beings that perform missions for God.

Maimonides felt that it is inconceivable that God would need help from independent beings. God created the laws of nature that accomplished all that God wanted, all that was needed, and all that was good. Furthermore, it is impossible to understand how such divine-like bodiless spirits could be seen by man. Just as God lacks any form, and therefore could not be seen, so, too, angels – who if they existed are said to be incorporeal – would be unseeable.

Maimonides discusses angels in his *Guide of the Perplexed* 2:6. He states there that angels exist – after all, the Bible mentions them – but the word should be understood figuratively. An angel is a force of the laws of nature: "every act of God is described as being performed by an angel." The word *angel* "means messenger; hence everything that is given a certain mission is an angel." Psalms 104:4 makes it clear that even the "elements are called angels, 'who makes winds, his angels.'" Maimonides explains that when Scripture mentions that someone saw an angel, it simply means that he had a dream or vision.

Maimonides maintains that his view is identical "with the opinion of [the Greek philosopher] Aristotle. There is only a difference in the names employed." Aristotle taught that the world functions according to the laws of nature and so did Maimonides.

## NACHMANIDES

Nachmanides disagreed. He was convinced that the world does not function according to the laws of nature. God is directly and daily involved in every occurrence on earth, even the most mundane, such as a leaf falling from a tree.

Nachmanides frequently discusses the ramifications of his belief in his Bible commentary; for examples, see his comments on Genesis 17:1 and 46:15, Exodus 13:16, and Leviticus 26:11. Thus, on Exodus 21:19 Nachmanides writes that only God, not doctors, can heal people.

Nachmanides argued that people can see angels. This happened, he wrote, in Genesis 16:11 when Hagar, Abraham's concubine, saw an angel. It occurred also to Abraham when he saw three of them in Genesis 18:2. Jacob wrestled with one in Genesis 32:25. Balaam encountered one in Numbers 22:31. Isaac was saved by one who appeared to his father Abraham and stopped Abraham sacrificing him in Genesis 22:11. These are just a few of many examples cited by Nachmanides.

He was also convinced that demons exist and that they interact with people. Since they can harm people, he outlined a method to avoid their harm in Leviticus 16:7.

### THE ZOHAR

Nachmanides's view also appears in such mystical works as the *Zohar*. The *Zohar* pictures Abraham accompanying the angels for part of their journey when they left him. "But, if Abraham knew they were angels," asks the *Zohar*, "why did he accompany them? Because he treated them like human beings."

### SUMMARY

Needless to say, one may believe as one chooses. Virtually any idea that one has about angels can find support in the view of some ancient sage. However, one should remember that ideas can have an impact upon human lives. They can encourage people to develop intellectually and motivate them to act to improve themselves and society. Alternatively, a belief that gives people the assurance that they are surrounded by protective supernatural forces can stifle people's behavior and induce them to be passive and indifferent, waiting for divine or semi-divine help, vegetating, instead of improving and aiding others.

# PART TWO

# CHAPTERS 3–16

# TALES OF THE JUDGES

---

*Chapters 3–16 make up the body of Judges. In these chapters, God punishes the Israelites for abandoning the divine commands but judges arise from time to time to aid the Israelites.*

---

**Chapter 3**

# *Did Ehud Act Properly?*

---

*This chapter contains four subjects. It begins with six verses that list the Canaan-ite and Philistine nations that Israel was unable to conquer because God allowed the nations to remain so that Israel could learn about warfare*[1] *and "to test Israel to determine if they would observe all of God's commands commanded by Moses." But the people of Israel dwelled together with these people and took Canaanite and Philistine women as their wives and gave their sons to the pagan women.*[2] *This introduction is followed by the tales of three of the judges; two stories are very short and the other long.*

---

OTHNIEL AND EHUD

As punishment for the Israelites' failure to observe the divine commands and their worship of idols, God "gave them over into the hand of…the king of Aram-naharaim…and the Israelites served [him] for eight years." The Israelites cried to God, and God sent them Othniel,[3] Caleb's brother, "upon whom was the spirit of

---

1. Rashi, Radak, and Gersonides felt that the Israelites needed to learn how to fight in the future because up to now they really hadn't fought. God fought for them and achieved their victories. These commentators also understood that the generation after Joshua failed to observe the divine commands because they did not realize that all the victories that Israel had attained in Canaan were the result of divine miracles.

2. Deuteronomy 7:2 forbids this behavior.

One could argue that these six verses (3:1–6) belong in chapter 2 and the tales of the judges starts with 3:7. The division of the biblical books into chapters was made by Christians in order to easily reference biblical verses. However, many chapter divisions do not make sense, such as the seventh day of creation appearing in Genesis 2 when logic demands that it belongs with the other days of creation in chapter 1.

3. He is also mentioned in 1:12.

God."[4] Othniel is considered the first judge. He "judged Israel"[5] and defeated the oppressors, the land was then quiet for forty years, and Othniel died.

Upon his death, the Israelites repeated their improper behavior, and the Moabites oppressed the Israelites for eighteen years.[6] The judge Ehud saved the people. His story is told in detail. The Israelites were faced with overwhelming problems. What could they do to save themselves from the overwhelming forces? How could they end their servitude? Would it be right to deceive their enemies and end their enslavement? Wasn't a preemptive strike the only way of saving themselves?

After careful consideration, Ehud, a left-handed judge with a crippled right hand,[7] decided that the only course open to him was to kill the king by deception. He took a short sharp dagger and hid it beneath his clothes on his right side. He then went to the king who was located on the eastern coast of the Jordan River and brought him a gift, which was most likely a demanded tribute.

He told the king that he wanted to tell him something secret from God. The king agreed to a private conversation, without suspecting that Ehud carried a dagger. He could not see it. He saw only a crippled man who could not use his right hand.

When the king rose to hear the message,[8] Ehud stabbed him, left the room and locked it. The king's officials thought the king did not want to be disturbed so Ehud had an opportunity to escape. When the officials saw that the king did not leave his room, they broke down the door and found the dead king. But it was too late to catch Ehud.

---

4. The Aramaic translation Targum Jonathan renders this "prophecy."

5. Boling (Anchor Bible, 1952) understands "judged" here as "mobilized" the Israelites for war, for this was a function of the "judge", and there is no indication that Othniel was involved in judicial matters.

6. Apparently only a portion of the Israelites were enslaved: Moabites controlled the area of Transjordan, where the two and a half tribes lived, and the area of Jericho – the only Canaanite territory that the Moabites conquered. The tribes of Benjamin and Ephraim lived in the conquered area of Jericho, and Ehud was from Benjamin.

7. Targum Jonathan understands the Hebrew to mean "crippled," but Rashi, Radak, Altschuler, and others state it could also simply mean that his right hand was as weak as a right-handed person's left hand.

8. Rashi and Radak understand that Eglon rose out of respect for God when he heard that the message was from God. They add that Eglon was rewarded for showing this respect by having as a descendant Ruth, the ancestress of King David.

While they were involved with taking care of the dead king, Ehud blew a trumpet,[9] gathered Israelite forces, attacked the garrison at Jericho, and defeated the enemy forces. "They smote of Moab at that time about ten thousand men."[10] Ehud and the Israelites did not enter Moab and did not take land from them; they only reacquired their own land. The Bible concludes the story by telling us that Ehud's actions secured peace for the area that lasted eighty years.[11]

## A CRITICISM OF EHUD

The Interpreter's Bible criticizes Ehud and the Israelites and charges them with barbarity. As I pointed out in chapter 2, ancient stories of Israelite battles and behaviors should be evaluated against those of other nations of the time, the mindset of the people, and the Torah attempt to elevate the nation.

The author of the Interpreter's Bible turned a blind eye to the biblical description of the dire circumstances of the Israelites, their eighteen years of abject servitude to a hostile nation, their need for deliverance, and the fact that combat was their last resort. He discounted the fact that Ehud and the Israelites acted with remarkable restraint. He overlooked the necessity of Ehud's deception given the overwhelming forces of the enemy.

Frequently, as the Chinese military sage Sun Tzu taught, the best or only military tactic is deception and surprise. It is often the only means to success and it secures the minimum risk of harm to one's forces.

Ehud's goal was to relieve his people from the Moabite yoke, not to secure a complete victory over his enemy. He fought only out of necessity and with restraint. He did not follow the tactic of the later German military writer Carl von Clausewitz, who taught the principle of continuity: pursue one's enemy with the utmost vigor without slackening the pace for a moment.

---

9. The Israelites sounded a trumpet for military and liturgical purposes (Numbers 10:9–10).
10. We will see the repeated use of this figure later in Judges. It should not be taken literally. It means "numerous." As mentioned previously, the Hebrew *eleph*, which means "thousand," could also mean military units; thus the translation would be ten units.
11. The Septuagint translation adds that Ehud judged the people until he died.

## SHAMGAR: JUDGE OR NON-ISRAELITE?

The land was peaceful after Ehud for eighty years.[12] After him was Shamgar the son of Anath who, presumably with helpers, "smote six hundred Philistines with an ox goad; and he also saved Israel."[13] The precise rounded number six hundred is obviously meant to imply "many."

Scholars note a number of interesting points in relation to Shamgar. The short story is told in a single verse. Shamgar is not called a judge. Absent is the general cyclical information: Israel did wrong, Israel pleaded to God, God sent a judge, the judge delivered the Israelites, and the land was at peace for a certain number of years. Shamgar's name is placed in 5:6 next to the non-Israelite Yael: "In the days of Shamgar son of Anath, during the days of Yael." Chapter 4 begins by stating that the Israelites acted improperly after Ehud's death; the chapter ignores Shamgar, seemingly implying that he did not judge the people. These details, together with the fact that Shamgar is not an Israelite name and Anath is the name of a pagan god, led many scholars to claim that Shamgar, like Yael, was a pagan who helped the Israelites.[14]

J.A. Soggin[15] suggests that it is possible to understand the story in this way: "Two people were trying to wrest the region from its inhabitants: Israel and the Philistines, and it would not be strange if one allied itself with the other, depending on the situation. So here we would have a Canaanite [Shamgar] allied with Israel against the Philistines, while in Judges 5 [when the situation changed] a Philistine is at the head of the anti-Israelite coalition."

---

12. This number, like ten thousand and forty, which appear frequently, should not be taken literally. It means a long time.

13. This is all we know of Shamgar. Gersonides and Altschuler suppose he was not very successful. As Altschuler put it, the reason Scripture does not say how long the land remained peaceful after his deed is because he did what he did in the year Ehud died and then died himself the same year. The story of Shamgar using an ox goad to kill Philistines is reminiscent of Samson killing Philistines with a jawbone of an ass in 15:16. The Philistines were a warrior people, well armed; however, Shamgar fought them with his work tools.

14. Such as J.D. Martin in the Cambridge Bible Commentary.

15. *Judges*, Old Testament Library (Westminster: John Knox Press, 1981).

## Chapter 4

# *Deborah and Discrimination against Women*

---

*Deborah and Samson are the most famous of the fourteen[1] or fifteen judges, and both are unusual – Deborah because she was a woman and Samson because of his wild behavior and superhuman powers.*

---

THE STORY OF DEBORAH

Judges 4 describes how Deborah, a prophetess[2] and judge, summoned Barak[3] to assemble troops to wage war against the Canaanites. Her story is retold in chapter 5 in poetry with apparent changes.

After Ehud, the prior judge, died, Israel resumed improper acts and God gave them into the hand of Jabin, king of Canaan, whose general was Sisera. Sisera had nine hundred chariots of iron,[4] and persecuted the Israelites for twenty years.[5]

Deborah tells Barak[6] that God commands him to fight Sisera. He agrees, but

---

1. If we consider Shamgar a non-Israelite. See chapter 3, where I note that some scholars say he was a non-Israelite. Some commentators, such as Rashi, add Yael as a judge, as we will see in this chapter. If so the number is fifteen or sixteen judges.

2. Radak states that we see no indication that Deborah prophesied after this incident; she was only given this power to solve this dire event. Did he say this because Deborah was a woman and he felt it was improper for women to lead men except under emergency situations?

3. The New Testament, Hebrews 11:32, lists Barak after Gideon, followed by Samson, Jephthah, David, and Samuel as those "who through faith conquered kingdoms," and does not mention Deborah. Is this author also disparaging Deborah because she was female?

4. The precise rounded number, like all such numbers, means "many."

5. Twenty, also a round number, signifies about half a generation.

6. Some commentators, such as Gersonides, suppose that it is possible that Barak was Deborah's husband because the verse states she was the wife of Lappidoth, which means flashing, and

only if Deborah accompanies him to the battlefield.[7] Deborah agrees but chastises him saying a woman, not he, will get credit for the victory. This cryptic prophecy may refer to Deborah being praised or to the non-Israelite Yael who slew Sisera after the battle.[8] Judges has Deborah ridicule Barak that a woman will best him. This fear of being surpassed by a woman is repeated in 9:54, where Abimelech fears that people will mock him saying that a woman killed him.[9]

Barak agrees to do as God willed. The Israelite force was made up of ten thousand[10] men (or ten military units) from just two tribes: Naphtali and Zebulun. They are successful. However, chapter 4 does not reveal how Barak achieved victory or whether he and his ten thousand men even fought. Verse 15 states: "And the Lord discomfited Sisera." The story of the battle unfolds only if chapters 4 and 5 are read in conjunction, for what is in 4 is not in 5, and vice versa.[11] However, as we will see, chapter 5 is filled with hyperbole and some of the events it describes conflict with what is narrated in chapter 4.

Sisera abandons his chariot and runs for his life.[12] He finds what he thinks

---

Barak also means flashing. In his commentary on verse 23, Rashi accepts the view of Targum Jonathan that Barak was a prophet.

7. But not to the battle itself. Why, asks Abarbanel, did Barak question Deborah's prophecy? He seems to think he will fail unless she accompanies him. Abarbanel answers that he did not question her prophecy, but wanted her to be present to help persuade the Israelites who might question what she predicted.

8. Yael was a Kenite. Chapter 1 states that the Kenites settled in the territory of Judah. However, 4:12 states that Yael's husband left Judah's territory and apparently aligned his family with the Canaanites. Despite this, Yael handed the Israelites their victory by killing the general. In the story only Yael was in her tent; we can only speculate what happened to her husband.

9. Abimelech led an army and besieged a city. "He approached the entrance to the castle to set fire to it. A woman tossed a millstone down upon his head and fractured his skull. He quickly called to his young armor bearer and said, 'Draw your sword and kill me, or men will say about me, "A woman killed him."' So the young man stabbed him and he died." This is another case of belittling women.

10. Another round number.

11. In 5:20–21, there are words indicating a flood. Scholars differ as to what this means. It could be describing a sudden unexpected rainstorm that muddied the ground beneath the chariots and made them immobile. This demoralized the Canaanites, who dismounted and fled. Barak's forces pursued them and according to 4:15 left none alive, "none" being a hyperbole. However, it could also mean that the water that Sisera's army was crossing suddenly flooded, similar to what happened to the Egyptians in Exodus 14 during the days of Moses.

12. He may have abandoned his royal chariot because it was mired in the mud or because he

is shelter in the tent of the non-Israelite Yael, but after offering him milk[13] and waiting until he falls asleep,[14] she kills him.

A third woman appears in chapter 5 – Sisera's mother, who stands by her window watching hopefully for the return of her son.

In 5:7, the poetic version of this tale calls Deborah a "mother." What is the author saying? There are several possibilities. A mother protects her children, and Deborah is protecting her people. This may be a literary device to contrast Deborah with Sisera's mother, who could not protect him. Similarly, the Bible sometimes calls large cities "mother cities"[15] because they protect the surrounding towns when necessary in a military manner, as did Deborah. However, the phrase calling her a mother fails to note that Deborah was a prophet and judge. Is it possible that this is still another denigration of women?[16]

## WOMEN IN JUDAISM

The Babylonian Talmud[17] lists seven female prophets: Sarah, Miriam, Deborah, Hannah, Abigail, Hulda, and Esther.[18] One opinion in the Talmud rates Sarah as a prophet superior to her husband Abraham. Many people read the Genesis tale and feel that the first female, Eve, was superior in intelligence and initiative to her passive husband Adam.

Yet, there were unfortunately many sages who read this chapter and made disparaging views about women. For example, Don Isaac Abarbanel asks: If Yael's

---

was afraid: his royal chariot was easily recognizable and when the Israelites would see it they would rush it and kill him. Some commentators think he ran by foot, others that he took a horse.

13. Some commentators translate the word as yogurt.

14. Chapter 4 seems to indicate that Sisera had fallen asleep, but some commentators read chapter 5's version as saying she killed him while he was standing, awake.

15. As in II Samuel 20:19.

16. Targum Jonathan changes the wording to "who prophesied concerning Israel."

17. *Megilla* 14a–b.

18. This view raises many questions. There is no indication in the Bible that the women other than Deborah and Hulda were prophets. And the Bible states that other women heard God – namely Eve (Genesis 3:13), Abraham's concubine Hagar (Genesis 16:17), and the mother of Samson (Judges 13:3). Why didn't the Talmudic sage include them? Did he exclude Hagar and Samson's mother because they heard God through an angel or because they and Eve only experienced a single prophecy? Did he exclude Eve and Hagar because they were not Israelites? What is the sage saying and why did he employ the oft-used number seven? We do not know. Is he arguing against those who minimized the value of women?

husband made a treaty with Jabin, king of Canaan, how could Yael breach that treaty? His answer: Women are not bound by treaties; they must only do what their husbands tell them to do. Abarbanel also questions why Deborah, a judge and prophet, needs to sit under a tree. The Aramaic translation of Judges, Targum Jonathan, answers that she dwelled in a house that was shaded by a tree. However, Abarbanel responds that she felt that it was inappropriate for a woman to be alone with a man in a house, so she arranged her meetings with men outside, under a tree.[19] The *Zohar*[20] reads: "Woe unto the generation whose leader [judge] is a woman." Several sources[21] state: "Prophetess though she [Deborah] was, she was yet subject to the frailties of her sex. Her self-consciousness was inordinate.... The result was that the prophetical spirit departed from her for a time while she was composing her song."[22]

Unfortunately, many rabbis even today insist that women cannot serve as judges. They explain that Deborah was an exception because of *hora'at sha'a*, the "extraordinary needs of the time." The rule states that sometimes a situation is so extraordinary that unusual steps must be taken to save Judaism or the Jewish people.[23]

YAEL

As with Deborah, various commentators made positive and negative remarks about Yael. We saw some negative views above. Since 5:6 lumps Shamgar with Yael,[24] many commentators opine that the two were non-Israelites, especially since chapter 4 specifically identifies Yael as a Kenite. However, Abarbanel and Gersonides take the opposite approach; both were Israelite judges.

---

19. Some Midrashim imagine that the judge Deborah sat under the tree where the patriarch Jacob buried his nurse also named Deborah. The Midrashim seem to imply that people considered the nurse's burial place holy and a suitable site for consulting a prophet. See sources in Louis Ginzberg, *The Legends of the Jews* (Philadelphia: Jewish Publication Society, 1901–1938), page 413.
20. *Zohar* 3:19b.
21. Babylonian Talmud, *Pesachim* 66b; *Zohar* 3:21b–22a; *Midrash Genesis Rabba* 40:4; and others. The quote is from Ginzberg 4:36.
22. There are dozens of other statements, pro and con, in rabbinical writings about women.
23. The rule is mentioned in *Midrash Sifrei Deuteronomy* 175; Babylonian Talmud, *Yevamot* 90b and *Sanhedrin* 46a; and Maimonides, *Mishneh Torah, Hilkhot Yesodei Hatorah* 9:3, among other sources.
24. "In the days of Shamgar ben Anath in the days of Yael."

Commenting on 5:24,[25] Ehrlich states that Yael bested Edomite women with her behavior, but not Israelite women who had a more developed culture and higher morals. Ehrlich castigates Yael for her murder of Sisera since he came to her tent seeking security, and she violated the ancient rules of hospitality.[26] Rabbi Johanan degrades Yael in the Babylonian Talmud.[27] He states that Sisera had sex with her seven times before she killed him because 5:27 describes Sisera's death poetically, using "sunk" and "fell" three times each and "lay" once, a total of seven times.

Neither Ehrlich nor Rabbi Johanan give Yael credit for handling an extraordinarily difficult matter well and for saving Israel.

In short, while the story of Deborah appears at first glance to be simple, it is actually quite complex. We really don't know exactly what transpired. Also, there are sages, rabbis, clerics, and scholars of all religions who disparage Deborah and Yael, some going so far as to minimize the humanity of women generally. But there are others who praise both women and recognize that women are people too.

---

25. "Blessed above women is Yael."

26. As the old man discusses in 19:5 and as Abraham's nephew Lot mentions in Genesis 19:8.

27. *Yevamot* 103a.

**Excursus**

# When Can We Ignore Laws?

---

*Chapter 4 raises the question: When can laws, even Torah laws, be ignored, and why did some prophets and other Jewish leaders do so?*

---

### THE NEEDS OF THE TIME

*Midrash Sifrei Deuteronomy* 175 and the Babylonian Talmud, *Yevamot* 90b, allow a prophet to act contrary to Torah law when the "extraordinary needs of the time" require it. Commenting upon Deuteronomy 18:15, which requires people to obey prophets, the Midrash and the Talmud state that one must listen to the prophet "even if he directs you to violate one of the commands recorded in the Torah – just as Elijah did on Mount Carmel [in 1 Kings 18] – obey him in every respect in accordance with the needs of the hour [*lefi sha'a*]."

What did Elijah do contrary to the law? Elijah engaged in a contest with the priests of the idol Baal on Mount Carmel: the priests and Elijah offered sacrifices, each to his god, with the goal of seeing which god would miraculously bring fire on the sacrifice. Elijah's sacrifice was offered outside the prescribed area, a prohibited act punishable by death. But it was permissible in this instance *lefi sha'a*, for in order to show that God is the true deity it was necessary to demonstrate to the Baal priests and Israelites that idols have no power to produce miraculous fire.

*Sanhedrin* 46a contains another example of necessity, *lefi sha'a*. It states: "Rabbi Eliezer ben Jacob said: I heard that the court may [when necessary] impose flagellation and pronounce [capital] sentences even when they are not [warranted] by the Torah. This is not done to disregard the Torah, but to make a fence around it [i.e., safeguard it]. It once happened that a man rode on the Sabbath during the

Greek era [when the invading Greeks ordered Jews to violate Torah laws]. He was brought before the [Jewish] court and stoned. It was not because he was liable [by law] to this penalty. It was done because of *hasha'a tzrikha* [it was required by the circumstances of the time]. It also happened that a man had intercourse with his wife [in public] under a fig tree. He was brought to the court and flogged [during this Greek period]. This was also not done because he merited it. Rather it was required by the circumstances of the time."

## MAIMONIDES ON *HORA'AT SHA'A*

Maimonides addresses the issue of *lefi sha'a* and *hora'at sha'a* and *hasha'a tzrikha*, terms expressing the same idea of "the times require the act," in several places. In his *Mishneh Torah, Hilkhot Yesodei Hatorah* 9:3, for example, he writes about prophets and repeats the law contained in the Midrash and Talmuds mentioned above: "When a prophet ... tells us to violate one or many of the Torah *mitzvot* ... it is a *mitzva* to listen to him. We learned this from the early sages, who had it as a part of Oral Law. ... We must accept his [the prophet's] decree in all things except idol worship according to the needs of the hour [*lefi sha'a*]. For example, Elijah [in 1 Kings 18] sacrificed on Mount Carmel, outside the Temple premises."

In his *Perush Hamishna* to *Sanhedrin* 6:2, and in his *Mishneh Torah, Hilkhot Sanhedrin* 18:6, Maimonides brings an extraordinary example. In Joshua 7, Joshua discovers through a vision that despite his order that no one should take booty from the defeated city Jericho, Achan did so. Joshua confronted Achan, who confessed to his crime. Joshua then executed Achan for the theft only by the authority of *hora'at sha'a*, since Jewish law does not inflict capital punishment upon a person who confesses theft or based on the testimony of a prophet who had a vision that the defendant committed the crime.

In his *Mishneh Torah, Hilkhot Mamrim* 2:4, Maimonides indicates that the power derived from Deuteronomy 18:15 was also given to a court without a prophet. A court may abolish a biblical law temporarily, but only as a *hora'at sha'a*, because of the unusual needs of the hour. If the court sees, as in the case of Joshua and Achan, that it is necessary to impress upon the public that a certain act can cause Judaism terrible harm, it may inflict corporal or capital punishment that is not sanctioned by the Torah as a temporary measure. Maimonides explains: this resembles a situation in which a doctor may see that it is necessary to amputate an arm or a leg in order to save a person's life. It is also like the rule in the Babylonian Talmud, *Yoma* 85b: one should desecrate a single Sabbath to save a person's life and make it possible for him to observe many Sabbaths.

Maimonides gives another example in his *Hilkhot Sanhedrin* 24:4. The religious leader Simon ben Shetah killed eighty women who practiced witchcraft in a single day, as indicated in *Mishna Sanhedrin* 6:4, even though women are not killed in this manner and a court may not kill more than a single person in a single day. This execution was necessary because the superstitious notion of witchcraft was widespread and was drawing the masses away from proper Jewish thought.

# Chapter 5

# *Biblical Poetry*

---

*Chapter 5 is the poetical version of the Deborah story. Many scholars[1] are convinced that it is one of the oldest parts of the Bible, and it was composed prior to the prose version in chapter 4. Like the poetic version of Joshua's battle in Joshua 10, the song version is filled with poetic hyperbole, such as the stars fighting for the Israelites, and with ambiguities, conflicting statements, repetitions, and words that can only be translated in a conjectural way.[2] Biblical songs are like poems that are filled with ancient illusions designed to prompt comparisons and arcane words that most readers do not understand. They are like eulogies that aren't offered to reveal the truth, but to praise and give thanks. They also resemble famous speeches such as Abraham Lincoln's Gettysburg Address and the final two speeches by Pericles to his city-state Athens during the first and second year of the twenty-seven-year Peloponnesian War against Sparta in 431 and 430 BCE: Lincoln and Pericles wanted to make their people feel good about their history and be inspired to prevail.*

---

## SPECIAL RULE FOR THE WRITING OF THIS SONG

The Talmud[3] states that Deborah's song should be highlighted by writing it in columns, as is Moses's song in Exodus 15. This distinction is not given to the other songs in Scripture. The biblical songs are: Moses's description of the miracle at the Red Sea in Exodus 15, Joshua extolling his victory at Gibeon in Joshua 10:12–13,[4]

---

1. For example, R.G. Boling in the Anchor Bible's *Judges*.
2. Twenty-two of the thirty verses have at least one word, often the key word, which is obscure (J.A. Soggin).
3. Jerusalem Talmud, *Megilla* 3:8, and *Masekhet Sophrim* 12:9–11.
4. While Deborah pointed to the stars as metaphorically helping the Israelites, Joshua used the sun.

Deborah's victory opus in Judges 5, King David's lament over the deaths of King Saul and his son Jonathan in 11 Samuel 1:17–27, King David's lament over General Abner's death in 11 Samuel 3:33–34, and King Solomon's praise and thanks at the dedication of the temple in 1 Kings 8:12–13. The consensus among scholars is that these compositions were created near the time of the events, perhaps long before the prose narratives of the events were composed, and they were originally transmitted orally.[5] It is possible that a collection of such songs appeared in a book called *Sefer Hayashar*,[6] from which the authors of the prose narratives drew them.

Some scholars add to the list of songs the entire book of Psalms. Others include the psalms of Hannah in 1 Samuel 2:1–10, of King David in 11 Samuel 22–23:7, and 1 Chronicles 16:8–26, and of King Hezekiah in Isaiah 38:10–20.

## WHO SANG THE SONG?

The thirty-one verses begin "Then sang Deborah and Barak," just as Exodus 15 starts "Then sang Moses and the Israelites." Virtually all commentators agree that neither Barak nor the Israelites were involved in the composition. At most the passage is saying that many people joined Moses and Deborah in offering praise and thanks. Barak is given virtually no credit for anything in chapters 4 and 5 – though the Greek translation of 1 Samuel 12:11 lists Barak instead of the Hebrew "Bedan," indicating that in addition to Jerubbaal (Gideon), Jephthah, and Samuel, Barak was sent by God to save Israel. Likewise, the New Testament ignores Deborah and considers Barak to be one of the judges in Hebrews 11:32.

## AMBIGUITIES

There are many ambiguous and obscure statements in chapter 5, in almost every verse. For example, the description of Sisera's military defeat in 5:20–22 is unclear: "stars in their courses fought against Sisera," the "river Kishon swept them away," "then did the horses' hooves stamp." Does this mean that Sisera's chariots were in

---

5. This could account for the errors that I will discuss further on.

6. Unfortunately, most ancient books and documents have been lost, including *Sefer Hayashar*. We no longer know what this book contained, but it seems to have listed ancient Israelite battles. 11 Samuel 1:17 states that King Saul's battle is recorded there. Numbers 21:14 mentions a battle described in the "Book of Divine Wars," which may be the same book. We also do not know the meaning of *yashar* here; it may be describing God or Israel as "upright" or "righteous," but it may also mean "song" or something else.

the Kishon when it suddenly overflowed and were drowned, as Pharaoh's forces at the Red Sea in Exodus 14; or were they on ground near the Kishon when the water overflowed its banks and mired the chariots in mud so they could not move; or something else? Does the mention of stars suggest poetically that God was involved in the battle, serve as a substitute word for heaven, or reflect the primitive notion that stars are the source of rain which flooded the river Kishon?

What is the meaning in 5:2 of "when men let grow their hair in Israel," describing what occurred just before the battle? Does it mean they grew hostile, reminding us of Samson's long hair and the practice of the military Greek Spartans who grew their hair long?

What is the significance of depicting God anthropomorphically traveling from Seir and Edom, the earth trembling, and the heavens dropping water in 5:4–5? Could this be a symbolic dramatic portrayal of the Israelites entering Canaan from the south?

"'You are cursed Meroz,' said the angel of the Lord" (5:23) seems to be Deborah's curse because Meroz did not come and aid the Israelites. But who is Meroz? Is it a city or person? Is it or he an Israelite or an Israelite ally? Who is the "angel"? Is it Deborah? Is the non-Israelite Meroz mentioned to contrast with the non-Israelite Yael who did help the Israelites?

REPETITIONS

Verse 19 is an example of the poem's poetic repetitions: "Kings came, they fought; then fought the kings of Canaan." Although the Bible abounds with poetic repetitions, even in prose sections, there are scholars who insist that the addition is supplying more information; in this case, that other Canaanite kingdoms joined Sisera to aid in dispelling the Israelite tribes from Canaan.

Verse 21 reads: "The river of Kishon swept them away; the river barred their flight, the river of Kishon." This may be a poetic repetition. However it may also be a conflicting account: the first phrase describes a flooded stream sweeping away Sisera's forces, but the second phrase seems to say they were unable to flee because their retreat was cut off.

CONFLICTING STATEMENTS

In 4:6 Deborah tells Barak to take ten thousand men (or ten units) from two tribes, Naphtali and Zebulun, and fight Sisera. Yet 5:8 mentions fifty thousand and verses 14–18 state that six tribes participated in the action while four others failed to respond and Deborah castigates them for failing to participate.

Chapter 4 describes a battle taking place in the north, while in chapter 5 it is further south, "although the two areas are united by the river Kishon."[7]

These verses seem to imply that the victory was the result of human valor, but 20–23 seems to speak of a divine miracle involving heavy rain.

Some scholars[8] see verses 26 and 27's seven-fold emphasis that Sisera sank down and fell at Yael's feet as a description of Yael hitting him while he was standing and drinking from a bowl. If so it seems to conflict with 4:21, she "drove the peg into his skull as he lay sound asleep."

## JUDAH

Judah (and Simeon, which was at this time part of Judah) is not included among the tribes that participated or failed to participate in Deborah's song. This may be another of many indications in Joshua and Judges that Judah did not consider itself part of the other tribes, ultimately leading to a Judean kingdom under King David from which the remaining tribes seceded after the death of Solomon. However it is possible that Judah's absence was due to this battle being part of a northern action in which Judah and Simeon, located in the south, had no interest.

## EHRLICH ON JUDGES 5

Arnold Ehrlich makes two tantalizing statements among his other comments. He asks: Why does chapter 5 focus on Sisera's mother mourning her son rather than Sisera's wife? He answers that it is natural for a mother to mourn a son's loss more strongly than a wife mourning for her husband. However it is also possible that the song's author wanted to contrast her with Deborah, who is called a mother in verse 7. The former sings joyfully while the latter laments.

Ehrlich also focuses on how Yael killed Sisera. She did not execute him with his sword piercing his heart or cutting his neck, which would have been a more honorable warrior's death, but in a degrading manner, with a tent-peg and hammer that pierced his temples.

---

7. J.A. Soggin.
8. J.D. Martin, the Cambridge Bible Commentary.

# Chapter 6

# *Gideon: The Hesitant Judge*

*Chapters 6–8 introduce readers to the judge Gideon. In chapter 6 he has several experiences that could be taken at face value and understood as supernatural events or as the internal struggles of an anxious man.*

## GIDEON'S INITIATION INTO LEADERSHIP

After Deborah's victory the Israelites lived in peace for forty years,[1] but as happened in the past and would happen in the future, the tribes lapsed into idol worship. This time, as a consequence, the Israelites[2] were harassed by Midianite[3] plunderers who for seven years rode into Canaan out of eastern Transjordan like "swarms of locust," bringing their families, cattle, and camels "past counting,"[4] and settled on the land until they consumed all of its crops.

A prophet comes and chastises the Israelites for their behavior. (There will be five revelations in this chapter: a prophet, an angel of the Lord, an angel of God,

---

1. Gersonides understands the verse to that say the land was at peace until the end of forty years, but the forty years include the twenty years of oppression. Thus the people had peace for only twenty years.

2. While this chapter and others seem to imply that every tribe was oppressed by the Midianites, it is more likely that the invading plunderers only attacked the area of some tribes. Thus later Gideon only summons help from three tribes (6:35).

3. There were helpful things the Midianites did for the Israelites as well as very harmful ones. People are not always good and a nation that is favorable to Israel doesn't assure that all its people agree.

4. Some scholars, such as William F. Albright, say that the Midianites were successful because they used camels. Some add that they were the first to domesticate these animals, but others cite evidence that camels were domesticated during an earlier period (J.A. Soggin, *Judges*).

the Lord, and God.)[5] The prophet reminds them that God saved them from Egyptian slavery[6] and from other oppressors. God had insisted that the Israelites not "stand in awe of the gods of the Amorites in whose land you are settling, but you did not listen to me."

Then an angel of the Lord appears to Gideon,[7] but Gideon does not know that the "man" is an angel. The Lord[8] speaks to Gideon, encouraging him to free Israel from the Midianites. Gideon claimed an inability to do so.

Gideon asks for a sign, his first of several requests for miraculous evidence that God is speaking with him. Gideon prepares a meal for the angel: a kid, unleavened cakes, and soup.[9] The angel of God tells Gideon to place the meat and cakes on a rock and pour the soup over them. The angel of the Lord touches the foods and a fire consumed them, despite the liquid. Then Gideon realizes that the man is an angel.

That night the Lord tells Gideon to take two bulls, one of which had to be seven years old, tear down the local Baal altar, and cut down the idol Asherah, the sacred tree standing by the altar. Gideon was then supposed to rebuild the altar and use the wood of the Asherah to offer the seven-year-old bull to God.[10]

---

5. The prophet is sitting under "the *eilah*." Although the definite "the" is used, the word could mean "a tree," but there are scholars who are convinced that the ancient Israelites considered some trees holy, and under the *eilah* would be a holy place. Gideon later builds his altar near the *eilah* in verse 24. The *eilah* is found in Scripture about a dozen times, including Genesis 35:4, Joshua 24:26, and Judges 9:6 (*Olam Hatanakh*).

6. The reminder that God saved the Israelites from Egyptian slavery is a constant biblical theme. Among much else, it introduces the concept of freedom for all people, especially when read with the biblical command, repeated thirty-six times, "You should love the stranger."

7. The angel's introductory words are "The Lord is with you mighty man of valor," giving Gideon assurances about the two matters that bother him: will God aid him in saving Israel and is he a proper leader. But he is not convinced.

8. It is not unusual for the Bible to describe a divine revelation as the appearance of a man or men, or an angel or angels, and then state that God, not the angel, spoke. For example, Genesis 18–19 relates that God appeared to Abraham, then states that three men appeared, and then, in chapter 19, identifies the men as angels.

9. Abraham did the same in Genesis 18:3–5. It is as if Abraham and Gideon are saying, "Eat first, then we'll talk."

10. This is the only place in Scripture where a seven-year-old bull is offered as a sacrifice. It happens here as a literary device to offer symmetry: the Israelites served Baal for seven years and were punished by Midianite cruelty during this period. They then showed devotion to God through Gideon's behavior by offering a seven-year-old bull as a sacrifice (Ehrlich).

Awakening, Gideon engages in his first battle, not against Midian but against Baal. Since he is still afraid, he and ten of his father's servants act at night, when people are asleep. When the citizens awake, they want to kill Gideon for destroying their altar. Gideon's father defends him and says in essence, let Baal do his own work: "If Baal is God, and someone has torn down his altar, let Baal take up his own cause." Then Gideon's father named Gideon Jerubbaal, saying "Let Baal plead his case against this man."

Meanwhile, several tribes join Midian for an attack. Gideon sends messages to four tribes calling them to join him to battle the invaders. Before the battle Gideon asks God to prove that he will "deliver Israel through me as you promised" by performing a miracle. Gideon requests that God make a fleece of wool wet with dew while all the surrounding ground is dry. God does so. Gideon then asks for a third sign – that God make the fleece dry while the ground is saturated in dew – and God does so.

### WHO WAS THE PROPHET?

This chapter raises many questions, chief among them being the prophet's identity. The book of Judges does not reveal the prophet's name. *Midrash Seder Olam*, Rashi, Gersonides, Abarbanel, and others say the prophet was Pinchas the grandson of Aaron, Moses's brother, who miraculously lived until this time. Gersonides adds that he was still alive during the reign of King David, as indicated in 1 Chronicles 9:20. Gersonides also accepted the view that Pinchas was still alive centuries later and was then called Elijah the prophet.[11]

Why didn't Pinchas act sooner? Why was there a need for Deborah to prophesy? Gersonides writes that Pinchas only acted occasionally.

### HOW DO WE UNDERSTAND THE FIVE REVELATIONS?

The chapter mentions five divine revelations, conveyed by the prophet, angel of the Lord, angel of God, Lord, and God. Are these different names for the same being, or five different divine beings? Commentators differ. Some say that each of these descriptions was a different kind of vision. Some claim that they are from

---

11. The legend states that God rewarded Pinchas with long life for killing the man and woman who openly cohabitated as part of a pagan idolatrous ceremony (Numbers 25:8).

different ancient traditions of stories patched together. Gersonides posits that they all refer to Pinchas, who was delivering God's message to Gideon.

It is possible to understand the chapter describing a natural, not supernatural, series of events. Gideon's internal struggle is similar to Jacob's struggle at the Wadi Jabbok in Genesis 32, where the Bible states he wrestled with a man, and Maimonides explains that it was a troubled dream.[12] Gideon recognized the danger and the need for someone to assemble the tribes to fight the Midianites, but struggled over whether he should lead. He felt that God was encouraging him, sometimes in one way, sometimes in another (each described in the chapter using another name: prophet, angel of the Lord, God, etc.). In his dream or thoughts he sought assurances. He thought he saw a sign, which made him confident. But then he wasn't sure, and sought more assurance, until he was satisfied.[13]

## DID GIDEON'S SACRIFICE ACCORD WITH JEWISH LAW?

The rabbis say that the Israelites were forbidden to make sacrifices in places other than the central altar. The sole exception is when the times required an exception. See chapter 4's excursus for an explanation of this rule and other examples of when exceptions are allowed.

## WHY WAS UNLEAVENED BREAD USED IN SACRIFICES?

Ehrlich notes that the Israelites joyously celebrated the upcoming deliverance from Egyptian slavery in Exodus 12 in a thanksgiving meal with special foods, including unleavened bread. He explains there that the ancients considered unleavened bread better than leavened bread. See "Why was the first Passover different from all other Passovers" in my book *Mysteries of Judaism*.[14]

## WHY ARE THERE MULTIPLE SIMILARITIES TO OTHER BIBLICAL STORIES?

Sigmund Freud[15] and others explained that dreams of distressed people are frequently filled with images from literature and legends that symbolize or express

---

12. In *Guide of the Perplexed* 2:42.
13. There are many biblical instances where heroes ask for signs, including Moses.
14. *Mysteries of Judaism* (Jerusalem: Gefen Publishing House 2014), page 27. Rashi writes that Gideon offered matzah because it was Passover.
15. *The Interpretation of Dreams*. See Robert Coles, ed., *Sigmund Freud: Selected Writings* (Book of the Month Club, 1952), pages 3–76.

their anxieties. Gideon was very concerned about his future and was therefore having dreams in which he visualized other people who faced his fears.

Gideon sees events similar to the events in the Samson story in Judges 13, such events being similar to stories in other cultures. Samson's father, like Gideon, is also visited by an angel who he thinks is a human; he offers the angel food, but the food is given as a sacrifice and burns miraculously. He then realizes he has been visited by an angel, and, like Gideon, thinks he will die because he saw an angel.

The story of the burning of the sacrifice to prove the existence of God parallels the story of Elijah when that prophet showed the priests of Baal that their sacrifice would not be accepted by God; in Elijah's case, a fire came down and took his offering despite it being drenched in water (1 Kings 18).

Gideon's struggles can be compared to other biblical stories:

1. The angelic appearance parallels Abraham's near sacrifice of his son Isaac in Genesis 22, which was stopped by an angel.
2. Gideon's angelic visitations also echo the tale of Abraham being visited by angels in Genesis 18.
3. Gideon's plea in verse 39 is nearly verbatim Abraham's plea in Genesis 18:32, begging God not to be angry as he speaks one more time.[16]
4. There are also similarities to the birth of Esau and Jacob in Genesis 25, where their mother sought an explanation from God and received it.
5. The reactions of Moses and Isaiah in Exodus 3–4 and Isaiah 1, respectively, when God appointed them for a mission, can be compared with Gideon's initiation into leadership.
6. The ten men that Gideon assembles to help him contrasts with the episode of Abraham pleading with God[17] to save the cities of Sodom and Gomorrah if there were ten righteous people in the towns. There weren't ten such people, but Gideon had ten supporters.

---

16. Gideon's destruction of his father's idols is the same as the legend of Abraham doing this same act, which is not in the Torah. It is a legend, probably copied from the Gideon tale.
17. In Genesis 18.

### WHY WAS GIDEON INSTRUCTED TO TAKE TWO BULLS BUT OFFER ONLY ONE?

After all his internal struggles, Gideon finally acts. Somewhat hesitatingly, he destroys the altar and Asherah at night when most people are asleep.

Gideon needed one bull to help pull apart the stones of the Baal altar and to uproot the Asherah tree. It would be improper to use a bull that would be sacrificed for this job.[18] We do not know what Gideon did with this bull after he sacrificed the other bull.

### IS IT PROPER TO REPEATEDLY ASK FOR DIVINE ASSURANCES?

It is certainly not proper to repeatedly ask for assurance from God, if one takes the story literally; once God states something we would expect that it is so. This is not a unique situation. Balaam in Numbers 22–24 makes repeated requests of God. If we understand the Balaam and Gideon stories as internal struggles, the question vanishes.

### WHAT WAS GIDEON'S BIRTH NAME: GIDEON OR JERUBBAAL? AND WHAT IS THE MEANING OF BAAL?

Gideon is called by this name eleven times in chapter 6, thirteen times in 7, and fifteen in 8; but he is called Jerubbaal once in 6, once in 7, twice in 8, eight times in 9,[19] once in I Samuel 12:11, and once in II Samuel 11:21.

The general meaning of *yeru* in the name Jerubbaal is "establish," suggesting that the combination means "Baal is established." However here it seems that *yeru* is understood as *yerab*, to "contest." Many scholars suppose that Gideon's name at birth was Jerubbaal and he was given the name Gideon as a result of this event, for the root of Gideon means "cut." He cut down the altar and Asherah. Gideon's new name also symbolizes his future battles against Baal.

During early Israelite history, Israelites used the name Baal, which means "Lord," as a name for God, just as we use "Lord" today, and many Israelites added Baal to their names, as we add El, "God," to many names today, as in Israel and Gabriel. Thus, Gideon's birth name does not necessarily indicate idol worship. Similarly, while the Israelites of Gideon's time worshipped Baal, this could have

---

18. Radak suggests that he took the bull so that the city inhabitants would not use it as a sacrifice to Baal.

19. Abimelech is always identified as the son of Jerubbaal, not the son of Gideon.

been a worship of God with religious syncretism, including some pagan practices in their ceremonies – a well-meaning but unacceptable behavior.

Around the time of King David, the use of Baal became unacceptable. The Bible mocks people who have names ending with Baal and substitutes *boshet*, "embarrassment," as in I Chronicles 8:33– 34; 9:36, 39–40; 14:7; II Samuel 2:2, 8, 12, 15; 4:4, 9, and more.

SUMMARY

There are essentially two ways to interpret chapter 6. We can accept the literal reading which has Gideon experiencing repeated supernatural encounters with God, or accept a natural and realistic interpretation, just as Maimonides did in the case of the encounter of Jacob with the man with whom he wrestled in Genesis 32:25–32.[20] Jacob and Gideon were facing the possibility of imminent danger and were afraid. During the night, each experienced their fears through dream images: Jacob wrestled with a man who symbolized Esau, and Gideon, in 6:11–26 and again in 6:36–40, sought God's assurances that he would succeed.

---

20. *Guide of the Perplexed* 2:42. Abarbanel disagreed with Maimonides's interpretation of Genesis 32 and understood that Jacob actually wrestled with an angel. He states here that while it is generally true that people cannot see or feel an angel, God can create a miracle whereby this becomes possible.

**Chapter 7**

# Gideon and the Three Hundred

---

*In this chapter the author presents a story with several themes: the number three, the consequences of fear, and the question of God's involvement in our lives.*

---

DIVINE MIRACLES OR NATURAL EVENTS?

A careful reading of the Bible reveals that despite the text apparently indicating that something occurred because of a divine miracle, the event happened naturally.[1] This chapter provides an example of this. The bulk of the chapter seems to state that the Israelites will be saved by the miraculous intervention of God, but its end shows that the people saw the victory as a natural event.

Gideon gathers forces to battle invading Midianites. God[2] tells him that he needs to winnow down the number of soldiers, for if a small force wins out against the 135,000 invaders[3] then people will realize that God brought about the victory. God suggests that Gideon tell all who are afraid that they should leave, and

---

1. Maimonides discusses this subject in his *Guide of the Perplexed* 2:48, where he explains that whenever the Bible states that God did something it should be understood as saying the event occurred naturally through the laws of nature that God created.

2. In chapter 6, Gideon experiences God in five different ways, probably indicating his agitated mind: a prophet, an angel of God, an angel of the Lord, God, and the Lord. Here, in chapter 7, it is only *y-h-v-h* in Hebrew, "Lord" in English. He is less anguished.

3. The Hebrew *eleph*, as I explained previously, could mean "unit," in which case there were only 135 units of enemy soldiers, with perhaps no more than ten men in a unit – a total of 1,350 invaders.

two-thirds of his soldiers do so.[4] The remaining ten thousand[5] is further reduced when God tells Gideon to have the soldiers drink from a stream and send away those who "go down on his knees and drink" but retain "every man who laps the water with his tongue like a dog." Those reductions leave Gideon's forces at three hundred men.[6]

As in chapter 6, Gideon is fearful. He doesn't beg God for a sign in this chapter, but it is implied or God sees that he needs something to give him courage. God suggests that he go near the Midianite camp where he will hear a conversation that will assure him of victory. Gideon takes his aide with him and overhears two Midianite soldiers discussing a dream.[7] An agitated dreamer says he saw a "barley cake rolling over the Midianite camp" and overturning a tent. The other interprets the dream as foretelling that Gideon's army will prevail.[8]

Gideon is assured. He returns to his camp and develops an offensive tactic. Each of the three hundred men is to take a jar and shofar,[9] and place a torch in

---

4. This seems to parallel Deuteronomy 20:5–8. However, the traditional interpretation of 20:5–8 is that the fainthearted, those who had just married, and those who recently built a home or vineyard are excused only for wars that are not *milchemet mitzva*, "divinely mandated wars" (*Sifrei Deuteronomy* 190; *Mishna Sota* 8:7; and Maimonides, *Mishneh Torah, Hilkhot Melakhim* 7:5). Gideon's battle is clearly divinely mandated and the fearful soldiers should not have been released. Why were they released? As we noted previously, the law may be ignored when circumstances demand it (see chapter 4's excursus). However it is also possible to interpret the events as follows: Gideon did not release the fainthearted entirely. He wanted to move forward with a small force. So he told the fainthearted to go away, but not far, for he would use them after he could frighten the Midianites and prompt them to run. This interpretation is supported by the fact that at the end of the chapter, Gideon summons soldiers from three tribes to pursue and kill the fleeing Midianites. It is unlikely that these were not men already near the battlefield, for it would take many hours if not days to mobilize these forces. So they must have been the men that Gideon had excluded from the three hundred.

5. Or ten units.

6. These three hundred fighters parallel the three hundred Spartans who fought at the Battle of Thermopylae in 480 BCE during the Persian Wars. Both stories show how a small group can obtain a victory over a numerically superior force.

7. The biblical Joseph in Genesis 41:25 also reflects the ancient notion that God reveals information to humans by means of dreams.

8. Scholars, such as J.D. Martin and G.F. Moore, interpret the barley cake as symbolizing Israel, for barley is a poor person's bread and a late crop, a crop that could be harvested after the Midianite plunder was completed and the marauders left. It is also the food of a settled community. The tent symbolizes nomadic people, such as the Midianite plunderers.

9. Abarbanel explains that shofars were available because in ancient times soldiers brought horns to battle and customarily blew them to terrorize the enemy. Ehrlich notes that Joshua also

the jar.[10] He divides the army into three groups and places them on three sides of the Midianite camp, leaving the eastern side open so that the enemy could flee into a trap. The troops approach the Midianite camp quietly during the second of the three parts of the night watch. At Gideon's signal they break the jars, creating a frightening clatter; reveal the light; and blast the silent night with the sound of the three hundred shofars. The surprised Midianites think that there are many soldiers surrounding them, perhaps a unit behind each light, and they flee east toward the Jordan to escape.[11]

Gideon summons three tribes to attack the fleeing Midianites and kill them. He also calls upon the tribe of Ephraim to cut off the fords of the Jordan so that the Midianites cannot cross. The operation is a success.

## FEAR

Fear is one of the themes of this chapter. It is emphasized by place names: Gideon's forces encamped at Ein-harod, which means spring of fright, and Ein-harod itself is near the hill of Moreh, meaning "fear." Fear is likewise highlighted through the release from service of all men who were fearful; God giving Gideon a sign to overcome his fear; Gideon fearing to look at the sign alone and taking his aide with him;[12] the frightened dreamer; the tactic to beat the Midianites by scaring them; and their fearful flight.

---

used the shofar to frighten the inhabitants of Jericho. He adds that since the shofar was used in ancient times to frighten one's enemy, we blow the shofar on Rosh Hashana to frighten and scare away Satan. Rashi understood that the soldiers blew their shofars to cause God to recall the merit they deserve for their ancestors accepting the Torah, for the shofar was sounded at Mount Sinai during the revelation of the Decalogue.

10. We can assume that usually each soldier wouldn't have a shofar, a torch, and a jar, but Gideon had the soldiers who left leave these items with those who remained.

Did the three hundred enter the battle without swords? It would seem so since their hands were full with three objects. No, Kaufmann contends, the swords could have been in their belts.

11. Psychological warfare, particularly the use of shofars to scare the superstitious enemy, was part of the tactic used by Joshua at Jericho. See my description of Joshua's tactic in my book *Joshua*, Unusual Bible Interpretations (Jerusalem: Gefen Publishing House, 2014), chapter 6.

When we recall that we are told at the outset that the Midianites came with their families and "camels as many as locusts," we can imagine that the Midianite superstition-induced flight must have been very confused.

12. It is possible to interpret Gideon's taking his aide with him as a usual procedure and not an indication of fear, for Jonathan, King Saul's brave son, did so in I Samuel 14, and he was not fearful.

## THE MEANING OF THE WATER DRINKERS

The book of Judges does not explain why those who stretched out and lapped water like a dog were chosen and those who bent their knees were dismissed, and the scholarly views vary, leaving it to the reader to decide.[13] Some opinions are:

1. J.D. Martin and others say that there is no significant difference between the benders and lappers: "The selection of which group is to remain with Gideon is made on purely numerical grounds." The goal was to have a small militia that would prove that the victory was accomplished by God; thus whichever of the two groups was smaller would remain.

2. Rashi, Radak, and Abarbanel see a religious explanation. They explain that the men who knelt showed they were accustomed to bowing to Baal, and God only wanted righteous soldiers.

3. Y. Elitzur notes that some consider the rejection of those who knelt as a symbol, indicating that the Judeans would no longer kneel to Midianites.

4. God typically chooses inadequate men to accomplish divine missions so that the result redounds to God's glory (Josephus, *Antiquities* 5, 6, 3).

5. Some commentators read the story as choosing the best warriors. Gersonides states that Gideon wanted the most able warriors and those who knelt were lazy.

6. The three hundred are compared to dogs: "They were rude, fierce men; compare the name Caleb," the warrior during the days of Joshua whose name may mean "dog" (G.F. Moore).

7. Those who lapped water did not put their heads into the water, but brought water to their mouths with their hands. They showed that even while drinking they were alert to a possible enemy attack (Kaufmann).[14]

8. Ehrlich and *Olam Hatanakh* take the opposite approach; Gideon chose the weakest group to show that the victory belonged to God. The lappers were

---

13. Jorge Borges (1899–1986) wrote: Great literature has two authors. It has obscure and ambiguous parts so that the tale is authored by both the writer and the reader.

14. Some scholars, such as Moore, suppose that there is a textual error here; the passage should read that those who lapped the water lapped it with their tongues, while those who were watchful knelt and brought the water to their mouths with their hands. The kneelers used their hands, not the lappers.

chosen because they acted in an unmanly manner, like dogs, not warriors, and no one could say such men achieved the victory without divine help.

9. The soldiers who bent down showed they were superior warriors, quick and courageous. Gideon rejected them because he wanted the weak, the lappers, to prove that the victory was God's (J.A. Soggin).

## THE USE OF SEVEN AND THREE

The Bible and other ancient literature and even fairy tales use the numbers seven and three frequently. In this chapter, the Lord speaks to Gideon seven times.[15]

The number three can be seen in the three hundred men, the three counts of Gideon's army,[16] the division of the three hundred into three units, the three items each soldier brings to the battle, the three parts of the night,[17] the three tribes called to pursue the Midianites, and the three stages of the battle: during the first watch Gideon has his forces take three items (verses 15–18), during the second watch the Midianites are frightened (19–22), and in the third three tribes join in defeating the foe (23).

## WAS IT GOD WHO DEFEATED THE MIDIANITES?

The chapter starts with the Lord telling Gideon that the object of the operation is to show that God secured the victory. Gideon's troop is specifically reduced to three hundred to show that with God's help a few can beat many.

Yet, there are indications that the victory was a natural event. The story begins with the appearance in 6:12 of an angel who states that Gideon is a mighty warrior. That occurrence suggests that the triumph will be achieved by Gideon's skills. Gideon gains the victory by using the psychology of fear. The tactic may have been God's advice, but the chapter does not say so. Once the Midianites began to run, chapter 7 does not suggest that God did something to them; it states instead that

---

15. The Lord is mentioned nine times in the chapter – in verses 2, 4, 5, 7, 9, 15, 18, 20, and 22. If the two battle cries by the military are removed from the list, the total is seven.

16. First 32,000 men (or 32 units). Second after the fearful men left, 10,000 (or 10 units). Then the reduction to 300.

17. The practice of dividing the night into three parts of about four hours each was changed by the Romans, who used a four-part division. See Exodus 14:24, 1 Samuel 11:11, Mark 13:35, and Babylonian Talmud, *Berakhot* 3a–b.

Gideon relied on three tribes who attacked them and the tribe of Ephraim who fought them at the Jordan fords. There were no miracles.

Furthermore, chapter 8 begins with the people of Ephraim criticizing Gideon for not sending for them sooner, presumably so that they could fight and gain more spoils.[18] That criticism suggests that they believed the victory was the result of human activity. Additionally, once Gideon sees that he is an accomplished warrior, he shows no fear in chapter 8, he needs no additional signs, and he no longer believes that he needs divine help.

The author of chapter 8 is presenting his readers with at least three ways to interpret his tale.

1. God is directly involved in all that occurs. While it may appear that humans bring results, it is actually God who does so.
2. Although God is not directly involved in controlling the events, God inspired Gideon in every action he took. The inspiration could have been by divine intervention, divine thoughts placed in his mind, or by Gideon being inspired by his view of God.
3. The story is composed with irony and addresses the common notion that God is ever-present and constantly involved in human activity. While it appears to people that this is so, and the narrator depicts it in this way in the first part of the chapter, the chapter's ending shows that it was not God but Gideon who attained the victory by using a psychological tactic and an unforeseen attack from the flanks on the confused, fleeing invaders.

---

18. Readers should pay special attention to the appearances of the tribes of Judah and Ephraim in the books of Joshua and Judges. The sanctuary was located within the borders of Ephraim, in Shiloh. Judah was the tribe that began the conquest of Canaan. A close reading will reveal that these two tribes have feelings of superiority. The clash between them ultimately resulted in the splitting of the united kingdom that existed under Kings David and Solomon and the creation of two kingdoms – the southern kingdom of Judah and the northern kingdom of Israel, led at first by Ephraim. This northern kingdom gets defeated by the Assyrians in 722 BCE, disappears from history, and becomes known as the ten lost tribes. Ephraim appears in Judges also in 5:14, when Ephraim did not aid judge Deborah; 12:1–2, in a contentious manner similar to here; and chapters 17–21, which contain a remarkable story.

Chapter 8

# Biblical Irony and Obscurities

*Chapter 8 concludes the three-chapter tale of Gideon. It affords us an opportunity, among much else, to see how the Bible uses irony and obscurities.*[1]

## GIDEON ON THE OFFENSIVE

Gideon successfully defeated the marauding Midianites. While chapters 6 and 7 depict a fearful Gideon depending on divine help, in this chapter he shows no fear, rather the opposite, and God offers no help. Gideon's men kill 120,000 armed Midianites, leaving an enemy force of only 15,000. For reasons unclear until the chapter's end, Gideon crosses the Jordan with his three hundred men[2] and chases the remnant Midianite force.[3]

Gideon's men need food. He requests food from the people of Succoth and

---

1. In the previous chapter I mentioned Jorge Borges's assertion that good literature – and the Bible is good literature – contains many ambiguities and obscurities. The result is that two people write good literature – the writer and the reader. Readers supply their understanding of what is not explicit in the text.

2. Gideon took only his three hundred men, and not the tribes that chapter 7 states joined him in defeating the plunderers. This led some scholars to believe that we have two tales here that are mixed together: in one Gideon wages all the battles with just three hundred men, in the other he uses a large force during part of his fighting.

Assuming this is a single tale, it is unclear why Gideon only took the three hundred. After frightening the Midianites in chapter 7, many Israelites joined him in the battle; why didn't they join him in the pursuit? We can only speculate. Perhaps the answer is that this was a personal matter, as we will soon see, and Gideon only took men of his tribe or extended family with him.

3. It is a common biblical writing style that Scripture describes an event without revealing crucial details until later.

Penuel.[4] Both refuse. We don't know why. Perhaps they feared that Gideon would be defeated by the Midianites, who had been successful warriors in the past. The Midianites would be furious if the cities helped their foe and would kill them. Gideon, the once fearful man, ignores their fear and swears that when he is victorious, he will return and punish the cities brutally. He surprises[5] and defeats the Midianite remnant, takes two Midianite kings prisoner, returns to Succoth and Penuel and fulfills his promise.

OBSCURITIES

What did Gideon do to the people of the two cities? The chapter describes different "punishments" – people of Succoth will be dragged over thorns as a threshing sledge is dragged over grain,[6] while Penuel's tower will be torn down. Are the descriptions metaphors? Are both treated differently? Why? Did he kill some or all of the inhabitants? Were they Israelites? None of this is clear.

There are many other questions:

1. Why did Gideon hunt the Midianite remnant?
2. Who told Gideon about the two kings, what they did, and where they were?
3. Why did Gideon say that if the kings had left his brothers alive he would not have killed them?
4. Why did Gideon lead his army without sufficient food in pursuit of the Midianites?
5. Who fed Gideon's starving troops?
6. This chapter states that Gideon captured the kings he had pursued, told

---

4. Ironically, both of these cities had significance in patriarchal history. Succoth, which means "huts," were the dwellings Jacob built when he returned to Canaan after an absence of some twenty years (Genesis 33:17). Penuel was where Jacob struggled with a man/angel (Genesis 32).
5. Gersonides supposes that Gideon used the same trick of surprise that he used in chapter 7, including the clatter of breaking vessels, lights, and shofar blasts.

The use of the military tactic of surprise rather than marching assuredly into the enemy camp is still another proof of what I discussed in chapter 7: the author's use of irony. While he began chapter 7 seemingly assuring readers that God would be involved in the victory and perform a miracle, he ends the chapter showing that no miracle occurred and Gideon relied on the human military tactic of surprise, as he did here.

6. The meaning of this punishment is incomprehensible, but seems to indicate a death by torture.

them he wouldn't have killed them if his brothers were alive, and then executed them. Why did Gideon say he would not have killed the kings if they had not killed his brothers … when there is no indication that he let other Midianites live?

7. Did Gideon wait to execute the kings until after he showed the people of Succoth and Penuel that he had captured them? Or did he bring them across the Jordan to expose them to the citizens of his hometown?

8. Why did Gideon tell his oldest son to kill the kings rather than doing it himself? Was this son a member of the original three hundred mentioned in chapter 7?

## POSSIBLE ANSWERS AND MORE ABOUT GIDEON

Rashi supposes that Gideon rushed to Transjordan without supplies to aid the tribes of Reuben, Gad, and Manasseh, who lived there. But many other commentators, such as Kaufmann, suppose that Gideon hastened to Transjordan to free his brothers who had been taken prisoner by the two kings. Gideon discovers that the kings didn't enslave them, but killed them. So he avenges his brothers' deaths by killing the kings. If the brothers were still alive and sold into slavery, he wouldn't have slain the kings, but would have traded them for his brothers.

Gideon may have selected his eldest son to perform the execution because he wanted his son to show he could succeed him as a fearless warrior king, but his son was weak and unable to do it, so he performed the execution.[7] This episode serves as an introduction to chapter 9 in which Abimelech, son of Gideon and Gideon's concubine, considers none of Gideon's seventy sons fit to rule.

The Israelites[8] offer to make Gideon king, but it is unclear who made the offer – was it one tribe, two, or all the tribes – and where the offer was made. Gideon refuses, but then acts like a king,[9] seemingly showing that his refusal was a ruse,

---

7. The weakness of Gideon's oldest son serves as an antithesis that highlights Gideon's strength (*Olam Hatanakh*). The rules of the blood vendetta are in Leviticus 24:17 and Deuteronomy 19:21. Gideon ignored these rules, which were enacted to limit revenge killings.

8. Actually the passage uses the singular, "an Israelite man." It is a very common biblical style to use the singular when the plural is intended and vice versa.

9. In kingly fashion, he takes many wives and has seventy sons and at least one concubine. The evil king Ahab also had seventy sons (II Kings 10:1). Is the author comparing Gideon to Ahab, for Ahab's wife killed a man to get her husband what he wanted?

a show of humility, a means of getting the people to push harder and become in-vested in the idea. Furthermore, if he became a king, what kind of king would he be, what would be his powers? Why didn't the author tell us, as he did for other judges, that Gideon judged the people? Even more significant, how should we understand this episode: Is the author showing his disdain of monarchy or the opposite, his feeling that the Israelites needed a king? This entire issue is obscure.

In chapter 6, Gideon's first action is the destruction of an idol. Yet in chapter 8, he requests the people to give him gold from the war spoils so that he can make an *ephod*, which he set up in his hometown.[10] What the *ephod* was is unclear. It could have been a monument to his victory,[11] an ornamental belt, or a kingly gar-ment. Whatever it was, the author tells us that despite the fact that Gideon began his career by destroying an idol, Gideon ultimately creates an item that "all Israel went whoring after," treating it as an idol. The chapter does not reveal when the "whoring occurred," during Gideon's life time or after his death. Rashi and Radak, apparently attempting to protect Gideon's honor, suggest the latter.

One of the characteristics of biblical writing is subtle references to other biblical events and people designed to prompt readers to make comparisons and thereby see both events and people in a much deeper way and clearer light. Gideon has seventy children and at least one concubine who may not have been an Israelite. We understand the number seventy to mean "many" and the taking of so many women of different types as an indication of royalty. King Solomon, another Israelite ruler, is said to have had seven hundred wives and three hun-dred concubines. Given that the numbers seven and three are frequently used

---

It is obscure whether the concubine was an Israelite, or like the women in Samson's life, a non-Israelite (as maintained by Moore). Her home in Shechem, where there were many non-Is-raelites, seems to indicate the latter. Verse 31 states that "he named [the son of the concubine] Abimelech ['my father is a king']"; it is unclear whether the "he" who did the naming was Gide-on or whether Abimelech gave himself this name when he made himself a king – for it was the practice of kings, as it is with popes today, to assume a new name when crowned.

The name Abimelech was also used by the king of Gerar in Genesis 20–21 and 26.

The number seventy should not be taken literally. It is used in the Bible to indicate many. A classic example is Exodus 1:5, which states that seventy people came to Egypt with Jacob, but a count reveals that there were less than seventy. The number of rulers and elders in Succoth is given as seventy-seven in verse 14, indicating a lot and even much more.

10. The donated gold weighed about seventy pounds.

11. In the ancient Middle East, many kings – Egyptian, Assyrian, Persian – would occasionally set up a pillar boasting of their conquests.

as approximations, we can understand seven hundred and three hundred as imprecise indications of exceedingly high numbers. The large numbers suggest that Solomon was more "successful" than Gideon. But should we see more from the comparison? Solomon was led astray by his foreign wives and built pagan temples for their idols. Is chapter 8 suggesting that Gideon was like Solomon in that manner? He too ended his life facilitating idol worship, probably unintentionally. This is yet another of the many ambiguities in this chapter.

IRONY

In this final chapter of the Gideon trilogy, we saw more than a dozen examples of obscurities and we examined one example of irony. There are other examples of irony, consequences contrary to what the author wanted us to expect when we began reading the chapter:

1. We saw the first example in chapter 6 when the author apparently wanted us to believe that the Israelite victory will be achieved only with divine help. The narration of the battle, however, shows that Gideon, who was fearful at first, was victorious because: (a) he initiated a surprise attack in which he caused the Midianites to be afraid and (b) he sought help from four Israelite tribes, not God, to overcome the fleeing marauders.[12]

2. In this chapter we see that the once fearful Gideon, filled with self-distrust, is now bold. The two kings recognize this and want to be slain by Gideon rather than by his son because it is more honorable to be killed by a bold man.[13]

3. We wonder whether Gideon has gone too far. In chapter 7, he shows humility in his magnanimous negotiations with the tribe Ephraim, but his treatment of Succoth and Penuel is harsh. Was his cruel punishment of the two cities justified? Although the text is obscure, it seems that he killed many of the inhabitants of the two cities, actions certainly not justified by today's standards. Additionally, did he act properly when he executed

---

12. This is one way of reading the tale. However, it is also possible to understand that Gideon acted by divine inspiration.

13. Radak and Kaufmann.

the two kings? Isn't that action still another ironic portrayal, a reversal of what we expected?

4. The author of chapter 8 tells readers that the names of the two captured kings are Zebah and Zalmunna. Those are likely not their real names. The author is using an ironic witticism: until they were captured they were kings, but now they are described as "victim" and "protection refused," the meaning of the names.

5. Another ironic episode is the request of the people that Gideon rule over them and be succeeded by his children. Yet, in the next chapter we will see the people participating in the murder of most of his sons.

Most readers of the prophetical books fail to see the obscurities and the ironies, and the humor in them. They approach the stories in an overly serious, even pedantic manner, unfortunately missing the author's clever art.[14]

---

14. The serious reading of the chapter is most likely based on the belief that the Tanakh contains the words of God, which the reader feels should be taken seriously. However, it is possible to see Scripture as the word of God presented with irony and witticisms.

**Excursus**

# *Comparing Gideon to Abraham*

---

*There are remarkable similarities between the Torah's descriptions of Gideon and Abraham.*

---

Abraham was visited by three angels in Genesis 18 and Gideon by one in Judges 6.[1] Both treat the angels as human visitors and give the angels elaborate meals and washing accommodations. Both serve meals for the angels under a tree. Each receives a remarkable prediction from his visitor(s): the birth of Isaac and the downfall of Midian.

Gideon smashes his father's idols in Judges and Abraham does so in *Midrash Genesis Rabba* 38:13. The latter tale is in all likelihood copied from the Gideon story.

Abraham defeats four armies with a force of 318 soldiers in Genesis 14:14–15 and Gideon triumphs over an overwhelming Midianite army with 300 soldiers. The two divide their almost same small number of men into divisions and both assault the enemy from all sides.

Gideon is the only judge whose name was changed. Abraham's name was also changed in 17:5.[2]

Both negotiate with God in a persistent manner, feel they are acting audaciously, and beg God not to be angry that they are persistent.

---

1. Maimonides, as I discussed earlier, considered angels to be forces of nature, anything that carries the divine will, such as rain and wind. Since physical or even "spiritual" angels do not exist, Maimonides considers these events to be dreams.

2. Other biblical figures also had their names changes. For instance, Jacob was renamed Israel, and Joseph was renamed Zaphenath-paneah by Pharaoh.

Abraham stops his petition to save Sodom and Gomorrah by speaking of ten righteous people. Gideon takes ten God-oriented people to aid him in smashing his father's idols.

The Torah states that both died *b'seiva tova*, in a ripe old age, in Genesis 25:8 and Judges 8:32. However, while Scripture praises Abraham for teaching God's ways,[3] the book of Judges ends its tale of Gideon by saying that he had made an *ephod* which became an object of idol worship. Thus Abraham left a pious legacy, whereas Gideon did not.[4]

---

3. In Genesis 18:17–19.

4. Despite what occurred to the *ephod*, an obscure item, there is no indication that Gideon intended it as an item of worship. He may have used it as a belt or a plaque. The misuse of a sacred item is not unusual. Moses stopped a plague by setting a staff in the area the plague had not yet entered, and this staff was later worshipped.

## Chapter 9

# *The Unexplainable Tale of Abimelech*

---

*The story of Abimelech, Gideon's son, is like a kaleidoscope with multiple forms and colors. Twist the handle one way and a picture appears, turn some more and another view emerges. The story contains more obscurities, witticisms, ironies, mistakes, and a remarkable parable.*

---

ABIMELECH'S RISE AND FALL

Gideon dies, leaving seventy sons. Abimelech, his son by his concubine, craves to be king. He persuades the people of Shechem, where his mother lived, to crown him as their king rather than be ruled by Gideon's seventy sons. With the aid of Shechemites, Abimelech murders every brother except the youngest, Jotham, who escapes. Abimelech is then crowned king.

Jotham interrupts the coronation ceremony. Standing on a mountain he berates the Shechemites with a parable that portrays Abimelech as a good-for-nothing person, a poor king, and a disaster for the people of Shechem and himself.

Within three years the Shechemites regret their decision and revolt. Abimelech wages war against them, and dies in one of the battles.

OBSCURITIES

As in the Gideon trilogy and numerous other biblical descriptions, chapter 9 is filled with obscure statements and episodes requiring readers to imagine what occurred. The different conclusions yield contradictory ideas of what transpired. Some obscurities are:

1. Did Abimelech behave properly when he killed his seventy siblings?

Though he failed to act according to modern standards of morality, he may have been following the ancient practice of removing competition to avoid being assassinated and assure a quiet reign. We know that King David advised his son Solomon, just before his death, to kill his opposition.[1] Was David acting appropriately? Perhaps Abimelech was a righteous judge with human faults.

2. How much territory did Abimelech rule: Shechem and its environs only, or also cities he attacked when they revolted against him?[2]

3. Was Shechem a Canaanite or Israelite city or a mixture of Canaanites and Israelites? Does the chapter show, as some scholars claim, that Canaanites and Israelites lived together?[3]

4. The chapter indicates that the Shechemites worshipped Baal and that their temple was called the temple of Baal. Was Baal an idol, its frequent meaning, or lord, the literal meaning? If the latter, it could refer to the Israelite God. Were the Israelites of this period and sometime later, or possibly just the Shechem inhabitants, worshippers of both the Israelite God and idols?

5. The chapter does not reveal Abimelech's argument as to why Gideon's seventy sons should not rule. Nor does it indicate whether the seventy were ruling at that time.[4]

6. Was Abimelech's mother, Gideon's concubine, a Canaanite? Was Abimel-

---

1. I Kings 2.

2. Although verse 22 states that Abimelech ruled over Israel, this is most likely hyperbole.

3. Y. Elitzur suggests that Shechem was a Canaanite city that did not fight against Joshua. It is not mentioned in Judges 1 as a conquered city. The Shechemites, according to Elitzur, usually humbled themselves before the Israelites, but did not forget their prior exulted origin in the days of the patriarch Jacob. Moore states: "Chapter 9 gives a glimpse of the relations between the two people [Canaanites and Israelites] thus brought side by side." He adds: "Many scholars see the story as a kind of prelude to the history of the kingdom of Saul" – both failed. The Interpreter's Bible agrees. Kaufmann and the Interpreter's Bible contend that the city was primarily Israelite and the chapter reflects an internal Israelite conflict, a civil war, a situation that had nearly flared up in the past and would do so in the future. If the city was Israelite, then Abimelech's mother was most likely an Israelite.

4. Perhaps Abimelech argued that it is better to be ruled by a single person rather than endure the confusion of having seventy rulers. If this was his argument then there is an ironic element here, for Abimelech created confusion.

ech half-Israelite? If so, what does this mean? Were Gaal and Zebul, who rebelled against Abimelech, non-Israelites?[5]

7. Did the people of Shechem agree to have Abimelech as their king and kill his seventy brothers because he was partially their kin, a half Canaanite? Did the people of Shechem later feel uncomfortable with that reasoning when they said he was the son of Gideon, at which time they felt that only a pure Canaanite should rule over them?

8. Some scholars[6] insist that when Abimelech heard that Shechem and surrounding cities were revolting against him and waged war against them, the author of chapter 9 mixed stories of two battles together. One is the tale of Gaal who led a revolt that was put down by Abimelech; Gaal was then tossed out of Shechem by the city administrator Zebul. It is in verses 26–41. The second tale tells about an uprising by all the inhabitants of Shechem. In that conflict, led by Zebul, Gaal is not involved. The Zebul story surrounds the one about Gaal, appearing in verses 22–25 and in 42 to the end of the chapter.[7]

9. Why doesn't the book of Judges identify Gideon and Abimelech as judges? The only other person whom some scholars consider a judge but who is not referred to as a judge is Shamgar, who some say was a Canaanite.[8] Perhaps the book is named Judges not because every person in it judged Israelites, but rather because that was the period "when the judges judged."[9] If so, the book describes some events that include people who were not judges.

---

5. Rashi writes that Gaal was a non-Israelite.

6. Such as J.D. Martin.

7. In verse 41, Zebul drives out Gaal from Shechem. Scholars who see 26–41 as a distinct tale of Gaal's revolt indicate that this is the end of the story; Abimelech defeated Gaal in battle; Gaal escaped to the city; and Zebul, who was in this tale on Abimelech's side, ejected him from Shechem. But then in verse 42 to the end of the chapter, Abimelech is fighting against Shechem as he did in 22–25. That sequence, they say, makes no sense. Zebul had shown allegiance to Abimelech in verse 41 by ousting Gaal.

Gersonides, who insists that the chapter is relating one episode, maintains that Zebul was trying to deceive Abimelech by banishing Gaal to make Abimelech think that he was on his side, but Abimelech saw through the hoax and attacked.

8. He is mentioned in two verses: 3:31 and 5:6. Although Shamgar is not called a judge, 3:31 states that "he also saved Israel."

9. This is the language of Ruth 1:1.

10. Why does the book not indicate that Gideon and Abimelech "saved" Israelites? It also fails to say this about Jair, Ibzan, Elon, Abdon, Samson, and Eli, and the description of Samuel is unclear. Was this omission intentional, to differentiate those people? If so, why?

11. How should we interpret Jotham's tale? Should we look for meaning in every detail? Is it a fable, parable, or allegory? What is the difference? I will discuss this tale below.

12. Is Jotham's tale a critique against monarchy?

13. Jotham delivered his castigation of Shechem and Abimelech from a mountain, presumably far enough away so that the people could not rush him, take him captive, and kill him as they did his brothers. How is it possible that the people of Shechem could hear him?[10]

14. The leaders of the Shechem community are called Baalei Shechem, meaning "*baals* of Shechem." Why is Baal used? It is an unusual appellation. Is it an ironic derogatory witticism that associates them with the idol, or does it simply mean "lords of Shechem," city leaders?

## WITTICISMS

1. Many scholars[11] note that the chapter's author uses *vayasar*, "And Abimelech *ruled* over Israel three years," instead of *malakh*, "reigned as a king,"[12] to downplay his role, as a disparagement and mockery.

2. The names in the Gideon and Abimelech stories seem to be descriptions of the individual's personality or activities, or insults. Jotham's name means "mourner"; he was the sole survivor of Abimelech's butchery of his seventy brothers. The name Gaal ben Ebed, who rebelled against Abimelech after the latter had ruled for three[13] years and who led the people of Shechem in a revolt until Abimelech defeated him, means "loathsome son of a slave."

---

10. Most likely the idea of a speech being delivered from a mountain is a literary device that should not be taken literally. The significance of mountains will be discussed below.

11. Rashi, Radak, A. Cohen, and others.

12. Verse 22.

13. As I have frequently pointed out, Scripture uses the numbers three and seven, including their variants when zeros are added, such as seventy. Seven and its variants suggest "many," while three and its variants denote "almost a lot."

Zebul, the administrator Abimelech placed over Shechem while he lived elsewhere, who also rebelled against him, was called "manure."

IRONY

The author shows more humor with his irony, such as:

1. Abimelech kills his seventy brothers claiming they were unfit to rule, but he was aided by "thoughtless and rash men" hired with seventy pieces of gold obtained from the treasury of the house of Baal.[14]

2. Shechem, the site of the rebellion against Abimelech, was a sacred place in earlier and later Israelite history. The Bible contains forty-eight references to that city; those references relate to Abraham, Jacob, Joseph, Joshua who buried Joseph in the area,[15] and Rehoboam. The latter rebelled against the Davidic dynasty, established his capital in Shechem, and called his country Israel.[16] Shechem, today called Nablus, is an Arab town in the West Bank of the Jordan River.

3. The people of Shechem crowned Abimelech their king but rebelled against him after a short three-year period.

4. Chapter 9 starts by mentioning women who bore Gideon seventy children and a concubine who bore him Abimelech; and it ends with Abimelech being killed by a woman.

5. The Shechemites did not select Abimelech because his father was the hero Gideon, but because they identified Abimelech with a woman, Gideon's concubine who lived in Shechem.

6. Abimelech is struck on the head by a millstone thrown or dropped by a woman. He tells his armor bearer to kill him because he doesn't want people to say he died a dishonorable death as a result of being killed by a woman.[17] His plan fails because the book of Judges portrays the true event

---

14. The use of the temple of Baal here could mean a sanctuary of an idol or one dedicated to the Israelite God. The story of killing seventy sons parallels somewhat the tale of the killing of the seventy sons of the evil king Ahab in II Kings 10:1–11. Each event depicts the end of an era, and much more.

15. Joshua 24:32.

16. While the kingdom under David's family was called Judea (1 Kings 12:1).

17. Abimelech's request is similar to that made by the two kings in chapter 8, who don't want to be killed by a young boy because it is dishonorable, and beg Gideon to kill them instead. It

for posterity. The episode is even mentioned later in II Samuel 11:21. Not only was he killed by a woman but she used a millstone, which was part of women's work in ancient times.[18]

7. In chapter 8, Gideon tells his "oldest" son to kill the two captured Midianite kings, but the boy can't do it. Gideon apparently wanted this son to succeed him. After Abimelech kills all but one of Gideon's sons, his "youngest" son Jotham confronts Abimelech with a fable delivered from a mountain.

8. Jotham says that the Shechemites and Abimelech will die by fire. He meant it metaphorically, but Abimelech burnt Shechem and was killed when he tried to burn another city.

9. Mount Gerizim from which Jotham narrated his fable is the same mountain upon which Joshua blessed the Israelite people.[19]

10. Trees play a repeated role in this story. Abimelech's crowning is by a sacred tree. Jotham's parable focuses on trees. Abimelech cuts trees to use as firewood to burn towns. And while he begins his reign by the sacred tree, he dies while trying to incinerate a town with trees he cut.

JOTHAM'S FABLE

There are many fables is the Torah that include animals and trees, such as II Kings 14:9 about a thistle and a cedar, and II Samuel 12 containing Nathan's fable about a rich man and a lamb. As well, I Kings 5:13 indicates that King Solomon composed many fables.[20]

Some scholars insist that Jotham's fable wasn't composed to castigate his half-brother Abimelech since none of the details in the fable fit the event. For

---

is also similar to King Saul's request in I Samuel 31:4: when he is dying of a wound inflicted during his final battle, he tells his armor bearer to kill him so that people would not say that non-Israelites did him in.

18. *Olam Hatanakh.* Abarbanel writes that Abimelech's desire to avoid being known as a man killed by a woman is "foolish." The embarrassment, he writes, only comes when a woman is able to overcome a man in combat, but being killed by a boulder thrown or dropped from a height by a woman is not shameful; "what difference does it make if thrown by a man or woman!"

19. Deuteronomy 27:12 and Joshua 8:33.

20. A fable is a short tale, often with animals or inanimate objects as characters. It is designed to teach a moral. An allegory is a figurative treatment of one subject under the guise of another. A parable is a short allegorical tale to convey some truth or moral lesson.

example, the fable speaks about the trees seeking a king and making the request first of the olive tree, second the fig tree, third the vine, and then settling on the thorn bush; but that description does not agree with what happened: the people of Shechem requested only one person to rule them, Abimelech. Other scholars recognize that it is characteristic for fables to have details that add spice to the story but nothing to its message.

Other scholars seek to find meaning in the three trees. Rashi says the olive tree represents the judge Othniel, figs Deborah, and vine Gideon. Gersonides interprets: oil symbolizes the oil used in the temple, wine an ingredient in sacrifices; he does not mention figs. Abarbanel criticizes this type of interpretation, saying, "What does this have to do with the episode!"

But Abarbanel also sees meaning in the three trees. He suggests that Jotham tells the Shechemites that they should have first tried to find a king, similar to olives, from the best families in the country. If this failed, they should have found a man who is rich, like figs, because a rich person shows skill in handling the economy. If such an individual was unavailable, they should have sought a man with a warm personality who treats others well, like the vine.

Kaufmann calls Jotham's story an allegory that suggests Israelite history, contains moral and political chastisement, and teaches about a proper monarchy.

## MOUNTAINS

Mountains play a role in the Jotham tale, in other Jewish stories, and in classical literature. *Olam Hatanakh* explains that the ancients considered mountains higher than the earth, close to heaven, a site for gods, such as Mount Olympus in Greek mythology. Mountains were considered sacred and were appropriate places for the burial of significant men, such as Aaron[21] and Moses;[22] the revelation of God's word;[23] and the transmission of blessings and curses.[24]

---

21. Numbers 20.
22. Deuteronomy 34.
23. Exodus 19–20.
24. For example, Numbers 21:20; 23:14–15; Deuteronomy 27:11–13, 33:15; and Joshua 8:33.

INTERPRETATIONS BY ARNOLD EHRLICH

Arnold Ehrlich offers a number of interesting comments on this chapter:

1. The donation of money to Abimelech by the Baal temple suggests that the priests supported him. Once the people saw that support, they joined the priests in siding with Abimelech, against the seventy other sons.
2. Those priests were pagans.
3. Jotham mentioned olives first in his fable because olive oil was used in anointing kings.
4. Jotham was prompted to deliver a fable about trees because he saw the Shechemites assembled at the sacred tree.
5. Verse 44 uses the word *v'harashim*, "and the units," suggesting that Abimelech had two units with him in addition to the two he sent toward the city. Given that the Israelites generally divided their armed forces into three units for battle – as in 7:16; 1 Samuel 11:11, 13:17; and Job 1:17 – verse 44 most likely contains an error. *Olam Hatanakh* agrees that our text is wrong and that the Septuagint word, based on a reading of *v'haanashim*, "the men," is correct.
6. Why did Abimelech kill his seventy half-brothers on a rock? The ancients believed the blood of a murdered person cries to heaven for revenge.[25] The divine punishment can be avoided by covering the blood with earth.[26] By shedding his brothers' blood on a stone, where the earth would not absorb it, Abimelech showed arrogant disregard of God who avenges crimes.

SUMMARY

There is no way we can assess with any certainty Abimelech's origin, personality, behavior, or success. He may have been a righteous judge who aided Israelites in many ways during his tenure as king, perhaps even controlling Canaanites in Shechem. Or, he may have been an egotistical unfeeling butcher who could persuade some of his coreligionists or Canaanites to accept his rule for a short time, until they rebelled. And he died a shameful death, egotistically bewailing the possibility that history would mock him for being killed by a woman.

---

25. As in Genesis 4:10.
26. Genesis 37:26 and Job 16:18.

**Chapter 10**

# "Minor" Judges

*This chapter opens by mentioning two men, speaking of one in two sentences and the other in three. It refers to both as judges, but does not describe their exploits. Chapter 12 (verses 8–15) continues by listing an additional three – providing two sentences about the first two and three about the third – but, again, there is no information about their deeds. Scholars call these five "minor" judges, not to belittle their accomplishments, but to indicate that the information about them is minimal. The description of those judges is thus similar to the minor prophets who, because of the shortness of their material, are collected in one biblical book, Trei Asar, "The Twelve."*

### THE CYCLE REPEATS

Chapter 10 ends with a description of the Israelites reverting to idol worship. God is angered and tells the people so.[1] God allows them to be persecuted for eighteen years by Philistines,[2] Ammonites, Zidonians, Amalekites, and Maonites.[3]

---

1. Radak, Gersonides, and others say the revelation was made by the priest Pinchas, grandson of Moses's brother Aaron. God's speech here is similar to the speech by the prophet in 6:7–10 and the speech by the angel in 2:1–5. None of these reproofs criticize the people for failing to obey Torah commands or offer any religious teaching; they only critique the people for worshipping idols.
2. Moore states that the reference to Philistines refers to a later period for "the period of Philistine supremacy began near the end of the time of the judges [Samson] and lasted until the days of David."
3. Two other nations – the Egyptians and the Amorites – are also mentioned as previous oppressors, which makes a total of seven nations. Scholars such as Ehrlich see "Maonites" as an error since there is no history of such oppression. The Septuagint substitutes Midian, the

The oppressed tribes cry to God admitting their misdeed, and God decides to save them.

Then the Ammonites encamp in Gilead,[4] preparing to attack, and the inhabitants of Gilead seek a man to lead their defense. Jephthah will appear in chapters 11 and 12.

WHO WERE THE JUDGES?

Let's recapitulate so that we can understand something about minor judges. Scholars differ regarding who was and who was not a judge. The largest suggested number of judges is seventeen. That number includes:

- Shamgar, who the book[5] states "also saved Israel," although he is not given the title "judge," and some scholars are convinced he was a Canaanite;
- Yael, who is identified as a Kenite;[6]
- Barak, Deborah's general, who acted only because of Deborah's insistence and who is not called a judge in this book;[7]
- two people who are not included in the book, Eli and Samuel.

If those five people are removed, there were twelve judges. It seems reasonable, however, to include Eli and Samuel since the book of Samuel refers to them as judges. Thus the number of judges is fourteen, five of them having only a sentence or two of description and no details of their exploits – hence the term "minor" judges.

There were apparently also judges who are not mentioned in this book. 1 Samuel 12:11 states that God sent Badan, Jerubbaal (Gideon), Jephthah, and Samuel to save the Israelites from their non-Israelite oppressors. Badan is not mentioned

nation Gideon fought. This is not the only apparent error in this chapter. *Olam Hatanakh* notes that the word for "cities" in Hebrew has a superfluous letter *yud*.

4. It is unclear if Gilead refers to the territory in Transjordan or to a city, and if so, which city (Kaufmann).

5. 3:31.

6. 4:17.

7. The Septuagint on 1 Samuel 12:11 reads "Barak" instead of the Hebrew "Badan," who with Jerubbaal (Gideon), Jephthah, and Samuel saved the Israelites from their non-Israelite oppressors. Also, the New Testament, Hebrews 11:32, lists Barak after Gideon, followed by Samson, Jephthah, David, and Samuel as those "who through faith conquered kingdoms." Both sources do not mention Deborah.

in Judges.[8] The Babylonian Talmud[9] states that Boaz of the book of Ruth was a judge, but identifies him as the judge Ibzan who is mentioned in chapter 12.

The book of Judges does not identify Gideon and Abimelech as judges and does not indicate that Gideon and Abimelech "saved" Israelites. The book also fails to make that same statement about Jair, Ibzan, Elon, Abdon, Samson, and Eli, and the description of Samuel is unclear. It is not known if those omissions were intentional, in order to distinguish those people.[10]

I suggest that the name of the book "Judges" is not intended to indicate that all the people mentioned actually judged the people, but rather that "this is the period when judges judged the tribes."[11] And the book includes events during this period with personalities and heroes who were not judges, such as Shamgar, and perhaps Gideon and Abimelech. I also suggest that the author or editor of Judges did not have all the relevant material about the people who lived and acted during that period, thus accounting for missing information. This understanding of the title also explains why the final section of the book – containing five of the book's twenty-one chapters – describes lawless events that occurred during this period, in which judges are not involved.[12]

---

8. There is an opinion in the Babylonian Talmud, *Rosh Hashana* 25a, that the book Samuel is referring to Samson, who is called there Badan because he came (*ba*) from the tribe of Dan.

9. *Bava Batra* 91a.

10. J.A. Soggin and others scholars acknowledge that they do not know how to explain why there is no information of the work done by the minor judges.

11. This is the language of Ruth 1:1.

12. Kaufmann states that it is possible that Abimelech saved Israelites during his three-year reign, but the description of these exploits were also lost. He supposes that the Samson narrative occurred before the time of Deborah. He reads 10:6–16 as a description of the end of Israelite worship of idols. He sees no indication that idols were worshipped during the time of Eli in the book Samuel, but idol worship resumed after Eli's death. Some might argue that there is no indication in Judges that the Israelites ceased the worship and that such a cessation would be contrary to human nature. The book ends with a tale of idol worship, and since a major theme of the book is idol worship one would expect the book to say that it had stopped if indeed it had.

## Excursus

# The Jephthah Saga – An Introduction

*The rather strange, often misunderstood saga of Jephthah begins at the end of Judges 10, in verses 17 and 18, continues in chapter 11, and ends in the middle of chapter 12, in verse 7.*[1]

### THE NATURAL PROGRESSION OF THE JEPHTHAH TALE

While many people like to believe that God manipulated biblical events and continues to do so today,[2] Y. Kaufmann stresses that the Jephthah tale is a realistic natural event. God, angels, and prophets are not mentioned, and there are no miracles or unusual events.[3]

*Olam Hatanakh* sees the Jephthah story as composed of seven parts:

1. The Israelites[4] face an imminent attack by non-Israelite forces.
2. The people appoint Jephthah to lead the Israelite army.
3. Jephthah tries to avert war by negotiating with the enemy.

---

1. Some readers will find this strange and will ask: Should the story have been placed in a single chapter? The answer is that the chapter divisions were not made by Jews but by well-meaning Christians who wanted to make it easier to find biblical writings. The problem with the division is that the person or persons who divided the chapters did not do so in a reasonable manner, as seen here. The classic example of this problem is the division between Genesis 1 and 2. Chapter one should have included the creation of the seventh day, but the divider placed it in chapter 2.
2. Nachmanides called this belief the greatest secret of the Torah. Maimonides was convinced that the opposite is true.
3. Another of many examples of this is the biblical book of Esther. But despite the absence of indicia of divine intervention, many people see hints in the texts showing divine intervention aiding the Israelites.
4. As usual in the book, "Israelites" is a hyperbole; actually the events happen to half of the twelve tribes.

4. He fails and war ensues.
5. Jephthah makes a foolish oath and fulfills what he promised.
6. Jephthah battles with the tribe of Ephraim.
7. Conclusion.

### DISHONORABLE LINEAGE

Jephthah is introduced to Bible readers[5] as a son of a prostitute: "and Gilead begot Jephthah."[6] Gilead is a large area in Transjordan. The verse may be telling readers that Jephthah's mother was so sexually promiscuous that anyone in Gilead could have been his father. We also read how in his early days, Jephthah formed a band comprised of vain fellows "and they went out with him,"[7] presumably doing bad things such as robbery. How could a person with such a background be chosen as a judge?[8]

A close look at Scripture reveals that his history is not exceptional. Jewish and Christian tradition states that the Messiah will be a descendant of King David, and David had an inglorious past and acted in an improper manner.

David's history begins when the patriarch Abraham's nephew Lot had sexual intercourse with his two daughters. They had two sons: Moab (meaning, "from my father") and Ammon ("my people").[9] Moab's descendant was Ruth the Moabite who married Boaz,[10] whom I will discuss shortly. The Moabites acted improperly with the Israelites during the days of Moses, and the Torah punished their descendants by forbidding Moabites from joining the Israelite nation.[11] However, this rule was later changed to allow the entry of Moabite women.[12]

---

5. In 11:1.

6. Gilead in this verse could be the name of Jephthah's father or refer to the Transjordan area.

7. 11:3.

8. 12:7 states that he judged Israel for six years.

9. Genesis 19.

10. Ruth 7:13.

11. Deuteronomy 23:4.

12. The rabbis homiletically say that Ruth converted to Judaism, but conversion did not exist at that time: Ruth did not go through any ceremony to make her Jewish, and she was always called Ruth the Moabite. Furthermore, the books of Ezra and later Nehemiah state that Ezra and Nehemiah criticized the Judeans for marrying non-Israelites and insisted that these husbands send their wives away. If conversion existed at the time (many centuries after Ruth), the non-Israelite wives could have converted, and Ezra and Nehemiah would not have required that they leave their husbands.

Boaz was a descendant of Judah.[13] Judah's son was conceived by Judah and his daughter-in-law Tamar, who Judah thought was a prostitute when he had sex with her.[14]

Like Jephthah, Ruth and Boaz's descendant David was a brigand and a robber before he became king,[15] and afterwards an adulterer with Bathsheba and a murderer of Bathsheba's husband, for which the Bible states God punished him by killing his first son with Bathsheba.[16] Yet, tradition states that King David was a wonderful person and is the progenitor of the Messiah.

The Bible is teaching that we should not judge people by their ancestor's acts or even their own past bad behavior as long as the people change.

### DID THE ISRAELITES KNOW MOSES'S TORAH?

There are several indications in the Jephthah story that Jephthah and the Israelites had no knowledge of Moses's Torah.

1. Jephthah's brothers expel him from their home in violation of Deuteronomy 21:16, which states that families must treat all children equally.

2. Jephthah vows that he will offer "whatsoever comes out of the doors of my house to meet me" as a thanksgiving burnt offering. This indicates that he intended to make a human, not an animal, sacrifice, for animals did not live in his house and come out of his doors to meet him. Human sacrifice is forbidden in the Torah.[17]

3. In recounting the history of Israelite encounters with Moab and Ammon, Jephthah mentions that Moses sent messengers to Sihon king of Moab requesting permission to go through his land toward Canaan. This story is not in the Torah.

4. The story is introduced by God stating that the Israelites will be punished because they worshipped idols, but there is no mention here or anywhere in this book that they were punished for violating the commands, such as the Sabbath, which are in the Torah.

---

13. Ruth 4:13–22.
14. Genesis 38.
15. I Samuel 22.
16. II Samuel 11–12.
17. Noted by Y. Elitzur and *Olam Hatanakh*. See also Genesis 22 and Jeremiah 7:31.

## MYTHICAL TALES OF CHILD SACRIFICE

The story of a father sacrificing his daughter is not unique to the Bible. In Homer's *Iliad*, which most likely predates the writing of Judges, Idomeneus king of Crete vowed to the god Poseidon during a storm at sea that if he returns home safely he will sacrifice to Poseidon the first person who greets him when he lands. His son meets him and he sacrifices him.[18] The *Iliad* also tells about the leader of the expedition to Troy, King Agamemnon, who vowed to sacrifice his daughter before the battle with Troy if Poseidon would stop the winds that prevented his ships from sailing.[19] These similarities led some scholars[20] to claim that Jephthah's tale is a copy of these earlier stories and the Jephthah events never happened.

We have no idea why the author of Judges included this bizarre tale of a human sacrifice. It is possible that he wanted to cause Israelites to sympathize with Jephthah's daughter and prompt them to cease copying the heathen practice.

The tribe of Ephraim complained to Jephthah that he failed to call them to engage in the battle against Ammon, probably because they wanted to share in the spoils. Previously they had issued a similar complaint against Gideon.[21] Unlike Gideon, Jephthah did not appease Ephraim with words, and unlike his own engagement with Ammon, he did not try to avoid war by negotiations, but started a brutal civil war. This together with his sacrifice of his daughter led many to consider Jephthah a bad leader.[22]

---

18. See also the play by Roland Schimmelphenning, *Idomeneus*.
19. See also the plays by Aeschylus, *Agamemnon*, and by Euripides, *Iphigenia in Tauris*.
20. See *Olam Hatanakh* to this chapter.
21. In chapter 8.
22. However, Radak, Abarbanel, Gersonides, and others claimed Jephthah did not kill his daughter; he required her to isolate herself and never marry, similar to the behavior of Roman Catholic nuns.

**Chapter 11**

# The Curious Story of Judge Jephthah

*Judges 11 contains a significant episode in the extraordinary life of the judge Jephthah: his sacrifice of his daughter. Jephthah was born in Gilead to a prostitute[1] and was apparently raised by his father or his adopted father, but his father's wife's children tossed him out of the parental home. He journeyed to another country where he was joined by a band of men who "went out with him," presumably engaging in illegal raids.*

## JUDGE JEPHTHAH

When the warring nation Ammon attacked the Israelites in Gilead, the elders rushed to the outcast and pleaded that he lead their defense, probably because of the skills that he had developed during his raids. Jephthah chided them for joining his brothers when they expelled him from his home. After further talk, he agreed to lead the battle if they would make him their ruler. The elders swore that they would do so, and the oath was announced publicly.

Jephthah tried diplomatic negotiations with the Ammonite king, which included a review of the history of the relations between the Ammonite and Israelite people, without success. Then, before going out to war, he swore an oath: "If the people of Ammon are given over to me, then whatever goes out from the door

---

1. The theme of a prostitute occurs often in Scripture. For example, Rahab is described as a prostitute who lived in Jericho and who aided the Israelites in conquering the city. The talmudic rabbis extolled her, and there is a Midrash that claims that Joshua took her as his wife. There is no indication that Jephthah's mother was also extolled. Just the opposite; he is presented as a man of humble origin who started life as a brigand.

of my house to me when I return in peace from the Ammonites shall be for the Lord. I will sacrifice it as a burnt offering."

Jephthah fought Ammon and was victorious. When he returned home, his daughter, an only child, greeted him with a victory ceremony, playing a musical instrument and dancing. Jephthah looked on in shock and tore his clothes in mourning. He told his daughter of his vow and insisted that he must keep it. His daughter agreed that he must do so. However, she requested that she be allowed to delay its execution for two months while she and her friends ascend the mountain and bewail her virginity. Then "he did with her according to his vow that he made."

## QUESTIONS

This story raises quite a few questions, including the following:

1. Why did Jephthah make his unusual oath?
2. Why didn't he nullify the oath when he saw what had happened?
3. What happened to his daughter?

## CAN THE QUESTIONS BE ANSWERED?

What makes this tale so fascinating is that the text itself offers no answers to any of these questions.[2] Both ancient and modern scholars suggest solutions, but their resolutions are no better than speculations. Readers should examine the story and seek their own understanding. They can view each detail from a religious, moral, psychological, social, literary, or other angle, if they choose. They may conclude that Jephthah was a terrible man or a righteous judge. They may want to consider the following thoughts:

1. The name Jephthah is derived from *patach*, which means "open." One can argue that with the opening letter *yud*, the first letter of God's name, it denotes "God opens." Ironically, chapter 11 relates incidences that are far from open and God is not evident in the tale.
2. The story concerns unnamed brothers who banish Jephthah, and he, in turn, banishes or kills (we will discuss this below) his unnamed daughter.

---

2. The Bible, as I mentioned in the past, is full of ambiguous and obscure statements and events.

3. With chapter 12, the narration depicts three family conflicts. Jephthah is evicted by his brothers, he cuts off his daughter and, in chapter 12 he kills ten thousand[3] fellow Israelites of the tribe of Ephraim.

4. Jephthah was selected to lead the people after the elders swore that they would make him their ruler. When the conflict with Ammon started, this oath by the elders, which affected his future status, was on his mind, and he made one of his own. Is it possible that he was afraid of breaking his vow lest the elders would see that they can nullify their oath? Or should we note that this explanation is unreasonable and even bizarre since by keeping his oath he would need to kill his daughter?

5. Offering a sacrifice in relation to a battle was a commonplace practice for many ancient people, and Jephthah was complying with this ubiquitous ritual. He may have been showing his reliance on and thankfulness to God. He may have expected that an animal would be the first to rush out to him when he returned, since the animals were in the field surrounding his home. Ironically, his daughter, following another long tradition, went out with ceremony to greet him, and met her disastrous end.

6. Women customarily greeted the returning victorious hero, and Jephthah should have known this when he made his rash vow.[4]

7. Jephthah's rash vow was not unique. Caleb made a rash vow in Joshua 15:16. He swore he would give his daughter in marriage to the man who would capture the town of Kiriath-sepher. It was rash because he had no idea who would conquer the town. Similarly, King Saul vowed to give his daughter to whomever was able to kill the giant Goliath.[5] Saul also vowed that the person who ate food prior to the victory against the Philistines should be cursed, not knowing that his son Jonathan would do so.[6]

8. Don Isaac Abarbanel, Gersonides, Radak, and Altschuler in his Metzudot David, cite the Babylonian Talmud, *Taanit* 4a, and the Midrashim *Genesis Rabba* and *Leviticus Rabba*, and suggest that Jephthah could have had his

---

3. The number ten thousand is a stereotype figure – as in Judges 1:4, where the tribe of Judah killed ten thousand Canaanites. It should be understood as "numerous."

4. Such as Moses's sister Miriam dancing and playing musical instruments after the victory at the Red Sea in Exodus 15:20.

5. David did so in 1 Samuel 17:50.

6. 1 Samuel 14.

vow annulled by the high priest Pinchas. However, Jephthah felt that because of his new leadership position he should not take the initiative and go to the high priest; rather, Pinchas should come to him. Pinchas, in turn, acted with equal hubris, demanding that because of his spiritual position Jephthah should travel to see him. Their arrogance resulted in the death of Jephthah's daughter.

9. The sages do not discuss the irony that both Pinchas (in the Torah) and Jephthah performed zealous acts for what they considered to be pious reasons, and some commentators[7] criticize both of them for their behavior – Jephthah for his vow and Pinchas for killing the man who had public sex during an idolatrous orgy without a judicial hearing.[8]

10. Some commentators[9] contend that Jephthah sacrificed his daughter as he had vowed. They say that the Bible does not state this explicitly – but uses the words "he did to her as he had vowed" – because it was considered too repulsive an act for the Bible to state openly.

11. Some of the commentators[10] state that although sacrificing children is strictly prohibited,[11] Jephthah and some other judges worshipped God together with idols and were so entangled with pagan notions that he did not realize that his act was wrong.

12. Some commentators,[12] relying on the Talmud and Midrashim, have an interesting contrary interpretation of the entire event. They contend that Jephthah never vowed to offer whatever exited his house as a sacrifice. By translating the *vav* in his final sentence as "or," instead of "and," which is its meaning in many verses, they understand Jephthah making a conditional promise: "I will sacrifice whatever exits my house if it is fit for a sacrifice. However [or], if it is unfit, such as a human or a dog, I will dedicate that item to God." Thus, since his daughter came to meet him, she had to be dedicated totally to God; that is, she had to live alone in a cloistered manner. In fact, Abarbanel suggests this episode as the origin and paradigm

---

7. See *Olam Hatanakh*.

8. Numbers 25.

9. Such as Rashi and *Olam Hatanakh*.

10. Such as Y. Elitzur.

11. As stated in Leviticus 18:21, 20:2–5; Deuteronomy 12:31, 18:10; and Jeremiah 7:31.

12. Such as ibn Ezra, Abarbanel, and Radak.

for the Christian idea to cloister females who would be perpetual virgins. Thus, he continues, Jephthah's daughter requested a two-month reprieve while she could wander around and see the world for the last time before she was secluded from society. She also asked for this time to "bewail her virginity." By this, she meant that she was bewailing the fact that she would never be able to see or marry a man in the future.[13]

## WHAT ANSWERS CAN WE GIVE TO THESE QUESTIONS?

It is instructive to realize that the sages selected Judges 11 as the haphtarah, the reading from prophetical books, to accompany the Torah reading of the biblical portion of Chukat. It is possible that Judges 11 was chosen as the accompanying haphtarah for two reasons:

1. Jephthah's negotiation with the Ammonite king focused on how the Israelites captured the land that had once belonged to the Ammonites from the Moabites, who had taken it from them. He referred to incidences that are recorded in the portion of Chukat. Thus the accounts are related.

2. Chukat deals with the obscure law concerning the "red heifer" which was used to purify an Israelite who became ritually unclean.[14] Both the laws of impurity and its nullification by using the dust of a burned red heifer are obscure.[15] Those who chose the Jephthah account as the haphtarah may

---

13. See Joshua Berman, "Medieval Monasticism and the Evolution of Jewish Interpretation to the Story of Jephthah's Daughter," *Jewish Quarterly Review* 95, no. 2 (2005): 228–256.

14. Numbers 19.

15. The Torah gives no reason why the ashes of a red heifer "purify" or "cleanse" a person who came in contact with a dead body. In his *Guide of the Perplexed* 3:47, Maimonides outlines four reasons for the laws of impurity. Even a cursory examination of his reasons shows that he was convinced that there is no spiritual basis for the laws.

First, he states, the laws of impurity "keep us at a distance from dirty and filthy objects." Thus, the ritual of the red heifer, which was employed when a person came in contact with a corpse, prevented – or at least somewhat minimized – the spread of infection.

Second, "they guard the sanctuary." By this he not only means that diseases are kept from the sanctuary, but contrary to the view of many others, Maimonides felt that frequent visits to the sanctuary would minimize its impact upon the person visiting it. Therefore the Torah established a number of impurity laws to reduce visits to the Tabernacle and later, the Temple, since an Israelite would frequently come in contact with "impure" objects.

Third, these laws reconfigure pre-Torah pagan notions of impurity and modify their rationale and practice, thus allowing them to be integrated into Jewish life.

have wanted to suggest that the story of Jephthah is as obscure as many laws in Chukat, and we can only guess the answers to the questions that the tale raises.

SUMMARY

The chronicle of Jephthah's remarkable life raises many imponderables, including why he made such an outrageous oath, why he failed to have the oath nullified, and how he fulfilled his outrageous vow on his daughter. The biblical text offers no answers. It does not even hint at a solution. One can only speculate.

It is possible that the sages selected the tale of Jephthah as the haphtarah of the portion of Chukat because they recognized that Chukat has laws that are difficult to understand. They wanted to highlight that the story of Jephthah is also obscure, but that it is worthwhile trying to unravel it.

---

Fourth, the Torah's impurity laws reduced the burden imposed by the pagan impure practices – which applied to all aspects of daily life – and restricted the impurity rules only to the sanctuary.

Thus the red heifer created no magic, neither did it remove anything since the "unclean" person was neither religiously nor physically dirty. It is possible that the red heifer was chosen simply because it added a lesson. It reminded users of the misdeed of their ancestors who worshipped the golden calf.

**Chapter 12**

# Why Didn't Jephthah Annul His Vow?

---

*Many people imagine that the Bible portrays its heroes in a favorable manner. Actually the opposite is true. Scripture portrays people with their faults. For example, Nachmanides claims that the patriarch Abraham sinned grievously in Genesis 20 when he traveled to Gerar and told its inhabitants that his wife Sarah "is my sister," to save his life from the lascivious Philistines.*

---

CIVIL WAR AGAINST EPHRAIM

In chapter 11 Jephthah didn't try to nullify his vow that he would sacrifice whatever came out to greet him when he returned from battle, and as a result he sacrificed his daughter. Most commentators, but not all, vilify him.[1]

In this chapter, the men of the tribe of Ephraim were furious because Jephthah didn't take them with him when he battled Ammon, perhaps because they were unable to share in the spoils of the twenty captured cities. They said, "We will burn your house upon you with fire." Jephthah replied that they hadn't helped his tribe during the nearly two decades when Ammon persecuted them, and so he felt he had to fight without them. Scripture does not reveal their reply. It is possible that they denied it and prepared to destroy Jephthah's house – meaning him, his family, and their possessions – and in self-defense, Jephthah preempted them and defeated them in battle. But this is speculation. We really don't know why Jephthah engaged in civil war.

Jephthah was successful. Some of the Ephraimites attempted to escape across the Jordan River, but Jephthah's men were there. The Ephraimites dissembled

---

1. *Mishna Nedarim* 2:1 and Jerusalem Talmud, *Pesachim* 9:6, state that Jephthah should have realized that his vow was a mistake and therefore an invalid vow.

saying they were not Ephraimites, but since Ephraimites were unable to say "Shib-boleth," and pronounced it as "Sibboleth," Jephthah's soldiers were able to expose their ruse. "There fell at that time of Ephraim forty-two thousand [people]." His behavior in these incidences seem to portray Jephthah in a negative fashion.

Let's look more deeply into one of these episodes. Why didn't Jephthah annul his vow? Everyone knows that people make hasty vows and there are religious ceremonies to annul vows, such as the recitation of Kol Nidrei at the start of Yom Kippur.

## JEPHTHAH'S VOW

Actually, Jephthah had no choice but to carry out his vow. Anglo-Saxon law allows the nullification of vows based on a mistake; so too does rabbinical law. Oath nullification, however, did not exist in the biblical period. The only nullification process that is mentioned in the Bible is in Numbers 30, which states that a father or husband can nullify a daughter or wife's vow.

This sole exception existed because the Torah considered daughters and wives to be the property of their fathers and husbands. What she has belongs to them and they control her vows. Even if she wants to carry out her promise, her father or husband can stop it. The only exceptions for females are widows and divorcees, who are no longer under male domination and whose vows, like those of men, cannot be rescinded. See my previous book in this series, *Joshua*,[2] for a more detailed discussion about the ancient view of vows.

---

2. *Joshua*, Unusual Bible Interpretations (Jerusalem: Gefen Publishing House, 2014), pages 88–91.

**Excursus**

# *The Rabbis Changed a Torah Law*

---

*We will explore the laws concerning vows more deeply here. Numbers 30:3 contains the divine command, "A man who vows a vow to the Lord or swears an oath, to bind himself with a binding obligation, must not nullify his word; he must do all that goes out of his mouth." This biblical law clearly forbids the canceling of a vow; once someone utters an oath, he must carry it out, even if it results in death. As I mentioned in the last chapter, this biblical rule forbidding nullification of vows was the view of all, or at least most, ancient people. The only cancellation process that is mentioned in the Bible is in Numbers 30, beginning with verse 4, which states that a father or husband can quash a daughter's or wife's vow.[1]*

---

### THE RABBINICAL HANDLING OF VOWS

The rabbis changed the law and allowed the abolition of vows. They interpreted Numbers 30 as stressing the significance of vows that had not been nullified, rather than forbidding nullification.

The fifth-century *Midrash Sifrei* understood Numbers 30 as speaking of the failure to carry out vows that had not been nullified. The Midrash stressed the sanctity of speech. It pictured the person who violated a vow that had not been annulled as a person who defiled a holy object.

The Babylonian Talmud, *Shavuot* 39a, understood the passage to be speaking about a false oath. The Talmud recalls that the whole world trembled at the time when God said at Sinai: "Thou shalt not take the name of the Lord thy God in

---

1. The laws of vows for men are also in Leviticus 5:4–5, Numbers 6, and Deuteronomy 23:19, 22–24. But this is the only site dealing with female vows.

vain." This is the kind of transgressor about whom the Torah says "The Lord will not hold him guiltless," meaning, will not leave him unpunished. And moreover, for most other transgressions of the Torah, the sinner alone is punished, but in this case he and his family are punished, meaning that a false oath generally affects other family members, and others suffer the same consequences.

The twelfth-century *Midrash Numbers Rabba* even warns people not to swear truthfully. "If a man says to his friend: 'I swear that I will go and eat a certain food at a certain place'... and even fulfills the oath, he will be destroyed. If this happens to one who swears truthfully, the consequences to one who swears falsely will be so much greater!"

The Midrash proves its point with an example. Alexander Yannai, a Hasmonean king who lived around 126–76 BCE, lost two thousand of his towns because, according to the Midrash, he swore a true oath. The Midrash states that people are only allowed to swear a true oath when three almost impossible conditions exist: (1) He must be as righteous as Abraham, Job, and Joseph. (2) He must devote all of his time to the study of Torah and the performance of its laws. (3) He must marry his daughter to a student who spends all of his time studying Torah and support him financially so that he does not have to neglect his studies.

SUMMARY

The Bible clearly forbids the nullification of vows by men but allows husbands and fathers to nullify oaths of wives and daughters since these females are under the control of their husbands and fathers. The Torah was reflecting the view of the ancients that vows are sacred and cannot be annulled. This ancient notion changed in many cultures and the rabbis accepted the change. As a result, despite Scripture's clear wording, the rabbis allowed the forgiveness of vows and interpreted the Torah mandate as an emphasis on performing what one promises to perform, unless the man cancels his vow.

**Chapter 13**

# The Inscrutable Tale of Samson

---

*Samson's story is told in Judges 13–16. The chapters twice state that he "judged Israel for twenty years": at the end of chapter 15 – before the episode of Delilah, after describing various episodes in which Samson seems to have violated what was later codified as rabbinical law, such as marrying non-Israelite women and killing people out of revenge – and at the end of chapter 16, after his death.[1] There is an additional third indicator of his service in 13:5, where the angel of God appeared to a barren woman telling her that she will bear a son, Samson. The angel states that the son "will begin to save Israel out of the hand of the Philistines," who were oppressing her tribe Dan and other nearby tribes at that time. Yet despite these indicators that Samson would judge and begin to deliver his people, there is no clear statement that he acted as a judge.*

---

NEGATIVE EVALUATION

Many scholars see Samson as a muscular, self-centered man, who was drawn to Philistine women and mischievous acts to his detriment. Even in his final prayer Samson does not think of his people, but of personal revenge. Rather than helping his people, his vengeful actions against Philistines who hurt him personally aggravated the relationship between the Philistines and Israelites. He did not stop the Philistine oppression; it continued unabated after his death. Unlike the other judges – with

---

1. Why was the number repeated twice? It is possible that we should view the Samson tale as occurring in three phases. In the first phase, until the end of chapter 15, Samson performed many improper acts. Then he matured in the second phase and judged the Israelites for twenty years; the events of these years are not recorded. At the end of the twenty years he relapsed and was enticed by Delilah. Chapter 16 ends by repeating that during his lifetime, he had acted as a judge.

the exception of Shamgar – he did not organize the Israelites to fight against the Philistines; all of his confrontations with Philistines were personal. His mother was told that he mustn't ingest intoxicating liquids and unclean foods,[2] but he engaged in festivities in 14:5 which may have included alcohol and unclean foods.

### HOW DOES SAMSON COMPARE WITH OTHER JUDGES?

I described in chapter 10 that the book Judges is unclear about many things, including how many judges judged Israel, the area and tribes they judged, and how they judged their people. Some scholars consider the number of judges to be as low as twelve and others as high as seventeen.

Samson was not unique in having unfavorable tales told about him. Abimelech and Jephthah also did evil things. Abimelech killed all but one of his seventy brothers and waged what may have been a civil war against Shechem and its environs. Judges ends its depiction of Abimelech's activities by saying, after describing his death, "Thus God punished the wickedness of Abimelech because of what he did to his father when he killed his seventy brothers." The book does not say that he judged the Israelites, although many commentators include him among the judges.

Jephthah killed his daughter according to the consensus interpretation or forced her to live a secluded life according to the minority opinion. He clearly engaged in civil war and killed forty-two thousand fellow Israelites. The book ends its narration of his activities by saying that Jephthah "judged Israel for twenty years." The evil deeds of these two men and those of Samson and the absence of any description of how they judged the people raise many questions, including: Does Scripture want readers to see these men as favorable figures? How should we understand the word "judges" since no description of their judgeship is given?

### SAMSON'S BIRTH IS FORETOLD

Samson is the only judge whose birth is foretold by an angel.[3] The predicting of the birth of a significant person is not unique to Judaism and is also found in other cultures. Genesis 18 contains the story of Abraham being told by three angels that

---

2. It is obscure what "unclean foods" refers to.

3. He is born after the Israelites reverted to idol worship and God gave them into the hands of the Philistines for forty years.

he will have a son. The New Testament has one angel foretell the birth of Jesus in Luke 1:30–31. Abraham received the message because he was an old man and the birth was unusual. Why were the other births prophesied? Is there significance in Abraham being visited by *three* angels?[4] Why did Samson's birth warrant the angelic prediction?

This was not the only sign that Samson's birth was wonder-filled and unique. His unnamed mother[5] was barren until the angel appeared, just like Sarah, Rebecca, Rachel, and Samuel's mother, who all bore important children.

A third sign of Samson's significance is that the angel instructed his mother to engage in unusual prenatal care, namely, to abstain from intoxicating drinks and unclean things, and "no razor must come on his head; for the child will be a Nazirite to God from the womb, and he will begin[6] to save Israel from the Philistine's hand."[7] Perhaps this maternal abstinence emphasizes that Samson was so important and his future acts so momentous that even his mother had to refrain from certain foods while she bore him.

Yet, the story portrays Samson as impetuous, with a choleric temper, and acting improperly – which do not seem to warrant miraculous antecedent events. Is it possible that this is irony: despite being assigned a divine mission, Samson did not carry it out? But are we reading the text improperly? Perhaps, as some scholars feel, we need to read the silences between the lines.

## WAS SAMSON SO IMPORTANT THAT THE PENTATEUCH PREDICTED HIS BIRTH?

Rashi wrote that the Torah predicted Samson's birth, but his grandson Rashbam disagreed. Rashbam criticized his grandfather's midrashic methodology with

---

4. The midrashic explanation on Genesis 18 is that every angel performs a single function. Abraham was visited by three angels, each of whom had a different role. One informed Abraham about the birth of Isaac, one destroyed Sodom and its environs, and one healed Abraham (Rashi on Genesis 18:2, based on *Midrash Genesis Rabba*).

5. The angel is unnamed. Only Samson's father is named in this chapter. Manoah, like Noah, means "rest."

6. Samson will begin but not complete the deliverance.

7. The laws of the Nazirite are in Numbers 6:1–21. A Nazirite is a man who vowed to abstain temporarily from intoxicant drinks and cutting his hair, but the Pentateuch does not indicate such a thing as a Nazirite from birth or a lifelong vow. However, Amos 2:11–12 speaks of a lifelong vow. The judge Samuel's mother petitioned God for a son and promised in 1 Samuel 1:11 that if she bore a son, no razor would cut his hair.

strong words in his commentary to Genesis 37:2 ("These are the generations of Jacob. Joseph, being seventeen years old, was feeding the flock of his brother, being still a lad, even with the sons of Bilhah, and with the sons of Zilpah, his father's wives; and Joseph brought evil reports of them unto their father") and 49:16 ("Dan will judge his people as one of the tribes of Israel"). In 37:2, Rashi explains each of the many phrases of the passage with a host of elaborate imaginative Midrashim that are not hinted at in the biblical words. He states that 49:16 is telling readers that Jacob predicted the judgeship of Samson, who was from the tribe of Dan.

Rashbam wrote in his commentary to 49:16: "Those [meaning Rashi and those like him] who explain that the verse refers to Samson do not know anything about the manner of interpreting Scripture's simple meaning. Would Jacob prophesy about a single individual who fell into the hands of the Philistines, who blinded him, and who died with the Philistines in a terrible situation!? *Chalila, chalila!* [God forbid! God forbid!]"

### HOW DID SOME RABBIS CONSIDER SAMSON RIGHTEOUS?

Some rabbis argued that Samson was granted an exception and allowed to marry a Philistine woman in Judges 14 because of a special need: he required an excuse to attack the Philistines. The marriage furnished Samson with just such a pretext: he attacked the Philistines in revenge for them taking advantage of his wife.

There are three times that the Samson story states that Samson was filled with the "spirit of the Lord."[8] Some rabbis, such as Rashi, interpret these references to mean that God was leading or directing Samson. A plain reading of the passages reveals that the phrase means "a strong impulse" or "feeling of strength." The first instance is simply saying that as Samson grew he showed his strength. The second and third are used to indicate that he exerted his strength to kill the lion and thirty men, respectively. There is no indication that God was involved. The same phrase is used in 3:10, 6:34, and 11:29, when Othniel, Gideon, and Jephthah go to war.

Rabbi I. Ginian[9] felt that God is involved in the daily life of humanity. God manipulates lives to accomplish the divine purpose; God punishes people if they do wrong, and may discipline an entire family or nation for the wrongs committed by

---

8. 13:25, 14:6, and 14:19.
9. In *Sefer Shoftim*, The Navi Journey (Kol Meheichal, 2010).

individuals because they should have stopped the person from doing the wrong. While some may read Judges as a book that occasionally portrays Israelite leaders in an unfavorable light, such as the story of Samson, Rabbi Ginian sees God working through the devout Samson to accomplish the divine purpose. Ginian ends his book by saying that the difficulty that some people have in maintaining faith is that although God is constantly involved in all that occurs in this world, God is invisible.

Ginian wrote that while the Bible states that the Israelites "did evil in the eyes of God" during the age of the judges, "the clear inference is that this was evil *only* in the eyes of Hashem [God]. Had we seen these people with our own eyes, we would not have perceived any evil." Yet, since the Israelites "underwent a general decline, sinking below the spiritual level expected of them…Hashem placed them under the domination of the small Plishti [Philistine] nation for forty years, something that in natural terms would never have happened."

After years of battles, Ginian writes, Samson fell victim to the Philistines because his father doubted the words of the angel who predicted Samson's birth. Ginian calls Samson's death the "far-reaching effects of errors." Samson never intended to tell Delilah about his hair, but God made him do it. Samson's father was a reincarnation of the biblical Noah and Samson of the patriarch Isaac's son Esau or, according to another view, a reincarnation of Moses's brother Aaron's son Nadav (whom God killed). The reincarnation afforded the souls of the deceased an opportunity to repair past errors and be purified.

Although unstated in the Bible, Ginian asserts that Samson did not sin by marrying a Philistine girl: the marriage was decreed in heaven, the girl converted, and the pair went through a Jewish wedding ceremony. God wanted Samson to marry this woman to begin Samson's war against the Philistines. This war was provoked when his wife was unfaithful to him and had an affair with one of the Philistines at their wedding ceremony.

Rabbi Steven Pruzansky had the same approach to the Samson story.[10] He felt that Samson was "the leading Torah scholar and spiritual guide" of his age. He taught his people Torah for some twenty years "between his skirmishes and intermarriages." His "one-man wars enabled the people to focus on rebuilding

10. In *Judges for Our Time: Contemporary Lessons from the Book of Shoftim* ( Jerusalem: Gefen Publishing House, 2009), pages 103–164.

their spiritual lives free from the terror of the Philistines." He explains that Samson married non-Israelite women as a two-pronged strategic subterfuge to ingratiate himself in the enemy camp and to seemingly separate himself from the Israelites so that the Philistines would not seek revenge for his deeds against his people.

Pruzansky explains that although Samson's strategy was directed by God, Samson failed because living among the non-Israelites turned his heart and mind. He fell in love with Delilah, whom he had been using as a tool to his task. Samson "was harmed by his prolonged exposure to the decadent society of the Philistines. He infiltrated it, but, in turn, it infiltrated him as well" even though he was protected by a divine plan and his Torah studies. This, writes Pruzansky, is a lesson for many Jews today who have well-meaning and seemingly cogent goals that fail because of the temptations of the non-Jewish secular environment.

In short, Rabbis Ginian and Pruzansky reflect the view of people who desire or need to see God functioning in this world and manipulating people as puppets to accomplish the divine will. None of this is clearly apparent in the book. A plain reading of the four chapters reveals Samson committing many improper acts.[11]

---

11. Abarbanel similarly felt that God sent Samson on his mission to begin the rescue of the Israelites from Philistine oppression, although Abarbanel probably did not believe that God was involved in every human action and thought. The name Samson is based on the Hebrew words *shamash*, meaning "serve" God's plan, and *shammam*, "destroy" (the Philistines).

Abarbanel explained that Samson was a Nazirite from birth, but different than the Nazirite mentioned in Numbers 6 and the descriptions in the Babylonian Talmud, tractate *Nazir*. The biblical Nazirite was a person who vowed to abstain from intoxicants and not cut his hair. Samson's abstentions were not voluntary, but a divine command. He was a Nazirite from birth. Unlike the biblical Nazirite, he had to abstain from unclean foods as well. Abarbanel wrote that Samson was not allowed to cut his hair as a sign of mourning for the oppression of his people. He had to abstain from intoxicants so that people would not imagine that his strength came from drink; they would realize it was from God.

# Chapter 14

# *Samson's First Amorous Escapade*

---

*Chapter 14 begins to describe Samson's strange behaviors. There are scholars such as Ehrlich who understand Samson to be violating biblical laws. Others, such as Abarbanel, Gersonides, Rashi, and Radak insist he is acting properly. Abarbanel argues that while Samson violated Torah laws he did so for a meritorious purpose, to exact revenge on the Philistines. Radak also insists that every act was proper – for example, his Philistine wife converted to Judaism. He writes: "Chalila [God forbid] that a judge in Israel should have sex with a Philistine woman and violate what the Torah forbids."[1]*

---

SAMSON'S FIRST ESCAPADE

The story of Samson's first erotic escapade is told in chapters 14 and 15, with chapter 16 depicting his encounter with two additional Philistine women. Samson sees a Philistine woman and informs his parents that he wants to marry her. They try to dissuade him from marrying a woman from "one of the uncircumcised Philistines."[2] But, the chapter continues, they "did not know that the Lord was doing this, seeking an opportunity against the Philistines, who were masters of Israel at that time."[3]

---

1. In Deuteronomy 7:3. This verse only prohibits marrying among the seven Canaanite nations, but the rabbis extended the prohibition to any non-Jew.

2. Some rabbis claim she converted prior to the wedding and went through a proper Jewish wedding ceremony. However the plain meaning of the text is that she remained a Philistine. In fact, conversion most likely did not enter Judaism until around 125 BCE. If conversion existed at the time, there would have been no reason why Samson's father would have disapproved of the marriage.

3. Some scholars are convinced that this sentence was added to the story in an attempt to show

Samson goes down[4] to visit the Philistine woman three times, the third time to his wedding ceremony. While traveling to see her during one of his earlier visits, he is attacked by a lion and kills it with his bare hands.[5]

The episode occurs far from the road and Samson tells no one what he did. During a later visit, he leaves the road to see the lion carcass and notices that a swarm of bees had entered the carcass and produced honey.

He comes to the wedding ceremony accompanied by thirty Philistines, who may or may not have been friends of his. That point, as many others, is obscure.[6] At the seven-day wedding feast he proposes to the thirty Philistines a riddle based on his killing of the lion: "Out of the eater food came forth, and out of the strong came sweetness."[7] He challenges that if they can unravel the riddle, he will give each of the thirty men a linen garment and a change of clothing. If they fail, they must give these items to him. They agree. They don't realize that it is impossible for them to unravel the riddle because the answer lies in an episode about which no one knows.

Frustrated because of their inability to solve the riddle, the thirty threaten

that Samson's acts were what God wanted. They point out that the story itself does not show divine intervention and, most importantly, God does not need an excuse or opportunity to act; if God wanted Samson to harm the Philistines, God could have directed him to do so based on the persecution they inflicted on the Israelites.

4. Radak notes that the rabbis derived a homiletical lesson from the phrase "went down": Judah went up to Timnah in Genesis 38 and the result was good. Samson "went down" and catastrophe ensued.

5. Tales about conquering lions appear in I Samuel 17:34–37 and II Samuel 23:20. They are also told in connection to the mythical Gilgamesh and Hercules.

6. There are several possibilities: (1) These Philistines were longtime friends of Samson, showing that he had somewhat assimilated into the Philistine culture. Ehrlich describes Samson as being overly attracted to women, without any interest in harming the Philistines. His relations with the Philistines changed when he saw how they treated him at his wedding. (2) They were people his proposed in-laws selected to join him in a kind of bachelor party to enhance his joy. (3) The Septuagint translation has a different wording: instead of the Philistines "seeing" Samson approaching them, they "fear him" because of his physical strength, and they appoint thirty Philistines to join him to make sure he causes them no trouble (Ehrlich).

7. Kaufmann, *Olam Hatanakh*, and many others note that Samson acted improperly; this riddle was impossible to unravel. The solution Samson was seeking was for the thirty companions to tell him how he killed the lion and later found honey in its carcass. Chapter 14 states that no one knew about the episode, so it was impossible for the Philistines to solve it. We have no idea why Samson acted as he did. Was this mischief, or an example of his disdain of the Philistines, or something else?

Samson's wife that unless she persuades Samson to reveal the solution to her and tells it to them, they will kill her and her family. She uses feminine wiles and persuades Samson to reveal the secret, which she tells them. Samson rages when they give him the solution. He pays them the thirty linen garments by killing thirty Philistines and taking their clothes, and then leaves his wife and rushes to his father's house. His wife is then "given to his companion, who was his friend."[8]

OBSCURITIES THAT CAN SHOW SAMSON AS PIOUS OR NOT

As previously noted, we could read the various episodes in this story as part of God's plan to give Samson an excuse to inflict revenge on the Philistines for their persecution of the Israelites or as indications of Samson's improper behavior. The following are examples of those episodes:

1. The thirty Philistine companions, as previously discussed, could have been Samson's friends whom he invited to his wedding, but there is no indication that he invited Israelites or even his parents. Did he not invite Israelites because he expected trouble between the Israelites and Philistines? There is no indication of that possibility in the chapter.

2. Did Samson violate his Nazirite behavior at the wedding feast by drinking and eating unclean food?[9] The chapter does not say that he did, but if not, what did he do while everyone else was drinking and eating nonkosher foods?[10]

3. Verse 4 states that Samson's parents "did not know that it [Samson's marriage to a Philistine woman] was of the Lord, for he sought an occasion against the Philistines." Should we understand that: (a) that statement was

---

8. How could the bride's father give Samson's wife to another man; she was married to Samson? Since Samson abandoned her, it was clear that he was angry at her, possibly even thinking she committed adultery with one of the companions, and the abandonment constituted a divorce (*Olam Hatanakh*). Abarbanel saw the suspicion of adultery in Samson's excited utterance to the companions, "you plowed with my heifer," although others understood that he only meant "you secured the riddle's solution from my wife."

9. The Hebrew word for feast, *mishte*, is derived from a root that means drinking because drinking was the primary element of a feast.

10. The Babylonian Talmud, *Nazir* 4a–b, explains that Samson was unlike the biblical Nazirite. He did not take a vow. He only had to observe the restrictions imposed by the angel in chapter 13, which did not restrict him from touching dead bodies.

added later to the description of Samson's madcap behavior, including murder, to show that it was part of God's plan; (b) that language was in the original text to show that Samson was carrying out God's will; (c) God provided the guidance for the overall plan to exact revenge on the Philistines, but Samson chose the specific method of implementation; (d) the reference "he sought an occasion" does not refer to God, but to Samson; or (e) the words "was of the Lord" do not suggest that God was involved, but mean it was a natural event, for God created the laws of nature?[11]

4. Samson acquires the thirty garments to pay the companions by killing thirty Philistines and taking their clothes. Was this proper? Radak states that Samson was doing God's will, so it must be right. Is he reading into the text what the text does not say?

## OTHER OBSCURITIES

1. The thirty companions answered the riddle: "What is sweeter than honey and what is stronger than a lion." But is this the answer to the riddle? It would seem that the only answer would be a description of Samson's struggle with the lion. Can we say that the chapter is only giving the introductory words of the solution, but the full solution is implied?[12]

2. Verse 15 states that the companions threatened Samson's wife on the seventh day, which seems to be a mistake since verse 16 states that she pressured him for seven days for the riddle's resolution. The Septuagint translation has the fourth day. Rashi states that "the seventh day" was not the seventh day of the feast, but Saturday. Is there a mistake in the text as Erhlich and others claim, and Rashi's interpretation is only a clever solution that is not hinted in the text?

3. Samson loses the riddle contest to the thirty companions because he is overwhelmed by feminine wiles. A similar event occurs with Delilah in

---

11. This is how Maimonides explains these kinds of events in his *Guide of the Perplexed* 2:48.

12. It would seem that the true answer would have had to be, "You are referring to when you killed the lion and later found honey from bees in its carcass." Some commentators say they did not want to answer the riddle exactly so as not to reveal that they forced Samson's wife to secure the answer from him. However, it is more likely that the chapter did not give us their full statement; this was only the beginning of their response.

chapter 17. Is the book telling readers that Samson's strength, although from God, can be overcome by a woman? Is this a reflection on what Eve did to Adam? Since "God's plan" is thwarted by a woman, does this support the view that the entire episode was not controlled by God but was a natural event?

4. Verse 18 states that the companions gave Samson the solution to the riddle "before the onset [or coming] of *hacharsa*." Rashi and others translate *hacharsa* as "the sunset," suggesting that they gave the solution before the day ended at sunset. However, Rashbam states that according to the Bible, the day starts and ends at daybreak, and the change to evening occurred when the Judeans adopted the Babylonian custom during their exile in Babylonia.[13] Without mentioning Rashbam, Ehrlich notes that *charas* is only used once in Scripture to mean sunset, and that is in a poem in Job 9:7 – and our verse is not poetry. He, Moore, and others suggest that there is a scribal error here and the original word was *hachedra*, "the bedchamber." The companions waited until Samson was about to lie with his wife before they surprised him with the solution.[14]

5. The winner of the bet was supposed to be given a linen garment and a change of clothing, but verse 19 states that he gave them only the changes of clothing. Should we infer that he gave both or that in his rage he paid only half what was owed, and the Philistines were too afraid to demand full payment?

6. Verse 20's *asher rei'ah lo* could be translated to mean that Samson's wife

---

13. Rashbam highlights this in his commentary on Genesis 1:5. The Torah states that God performed certain acts on the first day; then there was evening and then morning when the first day ended, and God began new activities for the second day. Apparently, the Jews changed the biblical practice during their exile in Babylon during the sixth century BCE. The temple ritual, however, did not change; sacrifices continued to start in the morning during the second-temple period.

14. Ehrlich suggests that they waited to the last possible moment so that Samson should not think they acquired the answer from his wife. However, it is possible that they waited until this important moment – the consummation of his wedding – to aggravate Samson. Moore cites scholars, including Josephus, who understand the chapter to be saying that Samson had not consummated his marriage until this time. Moore adds that this is the only instance in the Hebrew Bible "in which the bride remains in her father's house, and the husband lives with her or visits her there."

was given to the man "who had been his friend," as most commentators render it. However, Ehrlich understands *rei'ah* as "rival," as it is used in 1 Samuel 15:28. His wife was given to a man who had been Samson's rival for her affection prior to the marriage.

### THE OFT-REPEATED NUMBER THREE

The number three and its variations appear frequently in the Samson story.

1. The angel gave three instructions in chapter 13: not to partake of intoxicating drinks, not to eat unclean foods, and not to shave Samson's head.

2. The angel repeats his instruction of how Samson's mother and Samson should behave three times in chapter 13.

3. This is the third time that an angel appears to issue a prediction in the Hebrew Bible. The other two instances are to Abraham in Genesis 18 and Gideon in Judges 6. In all three of these instances three things occur: the appearance of the angel, the offering of a meal to the angel, and doubt about the prediction: Sarah doubted that she would bear a child, Gideon wanted another sign, and Samson's father did not believe his wife.

4. When Samson's father thought that he and his wife would die because they saw God, Samson's mother offered three reasons why this would not occur: God showed satisfaction with them by accepting their sacrifice, they were told that they would have a son which could not happen if they were killed, and God showed them the miracle of the angel departing in the sacrificial flame.

5. The book of Judges tells readers three times that Samson was filled with the "spirit of the Lord."[15]

6. Samson becomes involved with three Philistine women, to his detriment.[16]

7. Samson visits the first of the three women with whom he becomes involved three times.

8. The story of Samson's first sexual encounter can be divided into three parts:

---

15. 13:25, 14:6 and 19. While the Aramaic translation Targum Jonathan understands this as prophecy, Gersonides interprets as a feeling of strength.

16. The Babylonian Talmud, *Sota* 9b, states that Samson rebelled (*marad*) with his eyes and was punished with blindness; *lex taliones*, what we call "an eye for an eye."

The taking[17] of the woman (14:1–9), the marriage feast (14:10–19), and the disaster resulting in the end of his marriage (14:20 to the conclusion of chapter 15).[18]

9. Samson's companions, who were supposed to unravel Samson's riddle before the end of seven days, became frustrated with their inability to solve it after three days.

10. Samson is tricked by thirty Philistines and kills thirty Philistines to get their clothes.

11. Samson destroys Philistine crops by releasing three hundred foxes in the land with fire attached to their tails.

12. The Judeans send three thousand (three units) of their soldiers to capture Samson for the Philistines.

13. 16:2 uses three verbs to describe the Philistine reaction to Samson's visit to a prostitute in Gaza: they "compassed him" (surrounded him), "lay in wait" for him, but "did so silently" so he would not hear them.

14. Samson deceived Delilah three times before he told her about shearing his hair.

15. Radak understands Samson's second deception as binding him with a rope composed of three strands that would weaken him.

16. Three thousand Philistines congregate in the Dagan temple to see the humiliation of Samson; Samson kills them all.

---

17. In the Hebrew bible, the term "take" is generally used for marriage. The first time that the term "marry" (*nasa*) appears in the Tanakh is in Ezra 10:44; it also appears in Nehemiah 13:25, and II Chronicles 11:21, 13:21, and other Chronicles verses (*Olam Hatanakh*). The early concept of marriage was that it was consummated by the sex act.

18. *Olam Hatanakh*.

**Chapter 15**

# Samson Resumes His Amorous Behavior

*Chapter 15 is a continuation and conclusion of the first of Samson's three interactions with women. After abandoning his wife, he relents and decides to visit her. He brings a kid as a gift.[1] Samson's wife's father does not let him see her because he had given her to another man as his wife.[2] He offers Samson his younger daughter[3] and provoked a new series of revenge by Samson in a chapter filled with obscurities.*

---

1. Chapter 14 does not reveal whether he told his wife that he was leaving and informed her when he would return, or spoke to her at all, and whether he consummated his marriage. Scholars disagree on whether his marriage was the type we are familiar with, in which a wife leaves her parents' home and joins her husband; some scholars think this was an ancient kind of marriage in which the wife stayed in her parents' house.

   Samson brought his wife a kid. Some scholars (mentioned in Moore) humorously called this an ancient box of chocolates. Others (also in Moore) remind us that Judah, Jacob's son, sent a kid to the woman he thought was a prostitute, as payment for sex (in Genesis 38:17, 20, and 23).

2. He may have thought that by leaving his wife, Samson had divorced her.

3. The offer of a younger daughter in place of a promised older one is reminiscent of King Saul's act of promising David his oldest daughter, giving her to another man, and then offering his younger daughter Michal in her stead (1 Samuel 18:19). Unlike Samson, David accepted the exchange. This episode is also reminiscent of Genesis 29:20–23, where Jacob wanted to marry his beloved Rachel but her father substituted her sister Leah who Jacob accepted but still wanted Rachel. In the Jacob story the reverse occurs; the elder daughter is substituted for the younger one.

## FURTHER CONFLICT

Samson takes revenge for his father-in-law's deed with acts against all the Philistines. He attaches fire to three hundred foxes and releases them among the Philistine's corn, thus destroying their crop.[4] The Philistines react by burning Samson's wife and her father.[5] We do not know why they did so; they were innocents. Gersonides and Abarbanel speculate that the Philistines may have killed Samson's wife and her father with fire to appease Samson. They feared him and wanted him to know that they shared his outrage against his wife and her dad. Samson, according to them, is horrified by their gesture. He went out and killed many Philistines: "He smote them hip and thigh with great slaughter and then went down and dwelled in the cleft of the rock of Etam."[6] Etam was apparently within the land of the tribe of Judah.[7] Gersonides and Abarbanel are convinced that Samson acted properly; he was punishing the Philistines for their horrendous acts.[8]

But this was too much for the Philistines. A Philistine force left their land in western Canaan and encamped threateningly against Judah at Lehi.[9] They told the fearful Judeans that they wanted Samson. Unable to fight against the invaders, the Judeans sent three thousand men to capture Samson and bring him to them.[10] Samson agreed to accompany the Judeans on condition that they

---

4. This is similar to the Roman practice of tying torches to the tail of foxes during April in their Colosseum mentioned in Ovid, *Fasti* IV, 681. It is also like Hannibal's battle against Rome, in which he fastened fire to the horns of two thousand oxen and released them at night against the Roman military force.

5. The Septuagint reads "father's house."

6. This was the third attack by Samson, including what he did in chapter 14. It is not his last. The chapter does not reveal how many Philistines died.

7. We will read in a later chapter that the tribe of Dan, Samson's tribe, abandoned the Mediterranean area and settled in the north. (Although recorded in Judges later, it probably occurred before the Samson episodes.) Apparently some Danite families, such as Samson's family, did not join the trek north. Once the Danites left the area, some Philistines moved into parts of it from the west and some Judeans from the east. This explains why Samson did not flee to a Danite area but to one held by Judah.

8. Gersonides and Abarbanel, as well as many other rabbis such as Rashi, use this argument to also justify Samson's killing of many Philistines.

9. Actually the name Lehi, "jawbone," was given to the place after Samson used a jawbone to kill Philistines. However, it is customary for Scripture to foreshadow and call a place by the name it is given at a later time.

10. The term *alafim* can mean "thousands" or "units." Many scholars understand that the Judeans

do not try to harm him.[11] The Judeans tie him with two new ropes.[12] When he arrives at the Philistine camp, Samson is filled with the "spirit of the Lord."[13] He breaks his binds, finds a jawbone, and uses it to kill the Philistines.[14] The chapter concludes by stating that Samson "judged Israel in the days of the Philistines for twenty years."[15]

## USES OF THE NUMBER SEVEN IN THE SAMSON STORY

We saw in chapter 13 the ubiquitous appearance of the number three and its variations. The number seven also appears frequently in the Samson story:

---

sent three units, probably platoons. In any event, the large number that they sent shows that they feared Samson's strength.

Since the tribes were not united during this period and generally acted alone and pursued their own interests, the Judeans apparently had little qualm about handing Samson, a member of the tribe of Dan, to the invaders.

11. In the Pentateuch, the book Joshua, and the prior mention of Judah in Judges, Judah is always portrayed as being very strong. This is the first time that we see Judah as weak. Elitzur suggests that the Judeans at the time were being oppressed by the Philistines who dominated them. He also suggests that when the three Judean units saw Samson killing the huge number of Philistines, they joined him in the fray; however, this is not even hinted at in the text.

12. Ehrlich refers to II Kings 2:20 and contends that new items were used because they had magical powers, which the Judeans thought would counter Samson's strength. In II Kings, the prophet Elisha uses a new cruse to purify water. Martin cites I Samuel 6:7, where a new cart is used to carry the ark of the Lord, and says that new items are holy. While not exactly similar, Samson uses a new jawbone of an ass to smite a thousand (unit) of Philistines. The Hebrew word rendered "new" by the Jewish Publication Society translation is *teriyah*, which usually means "fresh." Samson found the jawbone of a recently deceased ass that had not deteriorated, was strong, and could be used as a weapon.

13. The Aramaic translator Targum Jonathan, Rashi, and others understand the phrase to mean prophecy, but the plain meaning in context is a feeling of strength.

14. Samson's use of a nonmilitary implement to kill his enemy is reminiscent of the act of Shamgar in 3:31, who killed three hundred Philistines with an ox goad.

15. Strangely, chapter 16 also ends with the statement that Samson was a judge for twenty years. Why is there this unusual repetition? *Olam Hatanakh* and Kaufmann suggest that the statement at the end of this chapter means that during the period after the events in chapters 14 and 15, and before those in chapter 16, Samson settled down and judged people for twenty years. At the conclusion of this period, he relapsed and had adventures with two other females, concluding with his death. The mention of the twenty years at the end of chapter 16 is simply the style of the book to conclude the story of the various judges by stating the length of their judgeship. Some texts of the Babylonian Talmud, *Sota* 10a, have the obvious error that Samson was a judge for twenty-two years. The Jerusalem Talmud, *Sota* 17:2, combines the figures of chapters 15 and 16 and states that Samson was a judge for forty years: even after his death Samson's deeds continued to impact the relations between the Philistines and Israelites for an additional twenty years.

1. At his wedding feast, Samson gave the participants seven days to unravel a riddle.

2. Samson fooled Delilah when he told her that he would be weakened if he were tied by seven fresh bowstrings that had never been dried.

3. Samson also deceived Delilah by telling her that he would lose his strength "if you weave the seven locks of my head with a web."[16] She fastened them together with a pin, but Samson retained his strength.

---

16. These braids were plaited to keep his long, unruly hair out of his face.

## Chapter 16

# *Samson's Death*

---

*The tragic death of Samson in Judges 16 evoked a positive reaction from the rabbis. They refused to condemn him for committing the forbidden act of suicide. Captured by the Philistines who blinded[1] and mocked him by making him stand as a ridiculous display in their temple, Samson prayed to God and "said, 'Let me die with the Philistines.' So he pushed with all his might and the house fell upon the lords and upon all the people that were there. So the dead that he slew at his death were more than they that he slew during his life." The rabbis saw Samson's act as a triumphal deed of leadership and martyrdom. Yet, despite the rabbinical reaction, a careful view of Samson's final days seems to contradict the rabbinical contention and reveals that Samson acted improperly.*

---

SAMSON'S SECOND PASSIONATE ADVENTURE

Samson travels to Gaza, has sex with a prostitute, and stays with her until the middle of the night.[2] A. Cohen[3] notes that Gaza "was thirty miles from Samson's

---

1. Just as the Babylonians did to King Zedekiah when they captured him (11 Kings 25:7).

2. The Hebrew word *zonah*, "prostitute," could also mean an innkeeper, and this is how Targum Jonathan, Abarbanel, Radak, and others see it: Samson came to a hotel and stayed most of the night. They say he did no wrong. Targum Jonathan, Rashi, Radak and others also translate Rahab the *zonah* in Joshua 2:1 as innkeeper.

The Interpreter's Bible, which often views Jewish history negatively, writes: "From our point of view, morals [at the time] were exceedingly low. But the writer shows no disappointment. Samson's morals were not out of the ordinary, and the storyteller obviously delighted in his process.... Samson faced enemies stronger than the Philistines. They were his own passions, his own careless disregard of the high gifts God bestowed upon him. And now his strength is to ebb away as he fails to use it for worthy ends."

3. *Joshua and Judges*, The Soncino Books of the Bible (Soncino, 1970).

hometown. For him to go to this place reveals the recklessness which was a trait in his character." Perhaps the fact that he went so far from home to visit a prostitute shows he did not want fellow Danites to know what he was doing.

The Philistines hear that he arrived and lay a trap for him.[4] They lock the gates of Gaza and await his attempt to exit the city in the morning, when they plan to capture him.[5] But Samson rises in the middle of the night,[6] finds the gates locked, rips them off their hinges, and carries the heavy gates together with all its parts on his shoulders to Hebron, "a distance of nearly forty miles" (A. Cohen).[7]

The episode with the prostitute provoked no retaliation by Samson since the Philistines did not harm him.[8]

### SAMSON FALLS IN LOVE AND DIES

Soon thereafter, Samson sees a third Philistine woman, Delilah,[9] and falls in love.[10] Representatives of the five Philistine lords visit her and offer to pay her a huge sum of money, eleven hundred shekels,[11] if she entices Samson to reveal the

---

4. They probably searched for Samson, but were unable to find him (Elitzur).

5. Ehrlich supposes that the Philistines did not want to attempt to capture Samson during the night lest they accidently kill the woman, a fellow Philistine.

6. Supposedly "in the darkness Samson slipped through their lines" (Moore).

7. The chapter does not reveal why he did this. Presumably to show his strength to the Philistines, to mock the Philistines who thought they could capture him, and to make it difficult for them to retrieve their gate. Many scholars doubt that even a strong man could accomplish such a feat and suggest that the Hebron where he deposited the gates was close to Gaza, not to be confused with the Hebron in Judah.

8. As pointed out in *Olam Hatanakh*, there is a literary connection between Samson's affair with the prostitute and with Delilah. He came to Gaza willingly to visit the prostitute, but was dragged unwillingly back to Gaza after he was weakened. In the first tale, he shows great power by carrying the Gaza gates; in the second he is weak and prays to God for strength. In the first, he holds the gates of the city; in the second he holds the temple pillars.

9. We have no idea what Delilah's name means. There are many speculations. Boling suggests "flirtatious," Martin "devotee" or "worshipper." For the rabbinical homiletical view, see the next chapter.

10. This is the first time that the word "love" is used in respect to Samson. Since this woman did not live in the Philistine territory, some scholars suppose she was not a Philistine, but a Canaanite. The chapter tells us nothing about her origin. Radak, Abarbanel, and others state that Delilah converted to Judaism.

11. Most commentators say that the sum is 1,100 shekels from each lord, a total of 5,500 – a huge sum that reflects the Philistine fear of Samson. Other commentators interpret the verse as saying Delilah would be paid 1,100 shekels which would come from the five lords, each paying 220. Some commentators think the sum 1,100 is strange; we would have expected a round number

source of his strength.[12] She agrees. During her first three attempts to discover the source of his strength, Samson tells Delilah he would lose his power if she did certain things to him. A careful scrutiny of these three acts reveals that they are associated with superstition and magic, attempts to dilute Samson's magic with stronger magic.[13]

The first attempt is to bind him with seven new bowstrings – seven was considered a magic number, and new objects were thought to have magical powers.[14] The second was to bind him with new ropes, which Radak explains were fortified ropes made of three strands (three being another magic number). Then Samson apparently begins to give in and for the first time mentions his hair. He told Delilah that if she weaves the seven locks of his hair into her loom, he would be weakened. Then, following three failures and constant needling, Samson reveals that his strength is based on his observance of the mandates the angel placed upon him, which include the prohibition against cutting his hair.[15] She shears his hair while he is sleeping and apparently binds him with the bowstrings described above.[16]

### IS IT TRUE THAT SAMSON'S STRENGTH LAY IN HIS HAIR?

Many rabbis and rational thinkers reject the notion that Samson's strength lay in his hair; it smacks of magic and superstition. The rabbis say that he was powerful only as long as he conformed to the angel's requirements.

We could interpret the episode as follows: When Samson told Delilah about the cutting of his hair, he must have known she would shear him – for when he told her the three other methods in the past, she tried them out. This may have

---

such as 1,000. However it seems that 1,100 was a customary usage at that time; it is used by Micah in 17:1.

12. They presumed that his strength came from magic since it was not normal. Samson mocks this notion by telling Delilah that the way to reduce his power is by counter-magic involving new items, for new items have magic, and by using the magic numbers three and seven.

13. Ehrlich reminds readers that even the Israelite prophet Elisha used a new vessel to miraculously purify water in II Kings 2:20.

14. These may have been "cords made from the intestines of animals" (Moore).

15. Chapter 13 does not record that the angel said Samson would lose his power if his hair was cut. Perhaps the angel did issue such a warning, but chapter 13 only relates the main points of the angel's instruction.

16. Other biblical heroes were imprisoned but rose from their confinement to greatness (Joseph in Genesis 41 and Daniel in Daniel 1–6), but not Samson.

been another of his deceptions, for he knew that it is nonsense to think that people are deprived of energy when their hair is shaven. But what he failed to remember is that his might came from God, and God would remove his power if Samson disobeyed the angel's rules. Thus, Samson told Delilah about his hair without fear that when he awakened from his sleep he would be weak.

When he woke, he knew that his hair was gone, but he said, "I will go out as other times, and shake myself [from the bonds that Delilah tied me]. But he knew not that the Lord had departed from him." The text is stating that his abilities departed because "the Lord had departed from him." It does not say, "because he was bald." Furthermore, the angel never says in chapter 13 that Samson's power would depart if his hair were cut.

Similarly, after being imprisoned for some time, until his hair grew back, this chapter does not say that his vigor resumed. Instead, it states that Samson prayed for the resumption of his might and it returned only because of his prayer.[17]

This understanding of the Samson saga assumes that God removed Samson's powers when Samson acted inappropriately. But this was not the first time he did so. We saw that Samson committed many improper acts, the most explicit being his sexual affairs with three Philistine women. The rabbis answer this critique by saying he always acted correctly until he met Delilah. His behavior with the women, they say, was designed to provoke an excuse to take revenge on the Philistines for oppressing the Israelites. Besides, forbidden sex was not prohibited by the angel. He is punished here for what the angel prohibited – the cutting of his hair – but the absence of the hair had nothing to do with the absence of his power. In regard to contact with the dead, the angel did not prohibit it; in regard to eating forbidden foods, there is no explicit statement that Samson did so.

In short, there are two ways to understand the Samson saga: We can understand the story as the rabbis say: he did no wrong until he met Delilah and allowed her to cut his hair despite the angel's instruction. God was involved in his life and helped him as long as he acted properly, and hindered him when he strayed from the divine will.

Alternatively, we can interpret the tale that God was never involved, the story

---

17. Abarbanel takes this approach: there was no magic associated with the hair; Samson was strong only when he obeyed God's will. Radak states the opposite; Samson's strength lay in his hair. He understands that Samson realized that his strength returned with the growth of his hair.

is filled with symbolisms,[18] and the episode of cutting the hair should not be taken literally.

## MISTAKES

I showed many examples of errors that crept into the biblical text over the millennia while the Bible was copied by hand. That fact does not detract from the sacredness of the text. Humans make mistakes even with sacred objects.

In this chapter, there are two verses in which words are missing. Verse 2 begins: "To the Gazites, saying." The verb is missing and is added in the ancient Aramaic and Greek translations "And it was told to the Gazites." So too several words are missing between verses 13 and 14. Verse 13 ends incompletely: "Samson told Delilah, 'If you weave the seven locks of my head with the web.'" And verse 14 begins in the middle of an action: "And she fastened it with a pin."

The Masoretes who fixed the Bible text during the second half of the first millennium noted five misspellings in the chapter.[19]

## THE MOCKING OF SAMSON

Samson destroyed the crop of the Philistines in chapter 15 by placing fire on the tails of three hundred foxes. The Philistines made him pay for this deed tit for tat; he was forced to do work generally assigned to women, grinding their grain. Later they brought him to the temple of their god Dagan, whose name is variously defined, but most commentators understand that it means "corn."[20]

---

18. For many events in the story are impossible. For example, how could Samson reach the two pillars that held up the Dagan temple, given that pillars that hold up a building that can contain thirty thousand people must be far apart? How could Samson unhinge Gaza's gate – a complex structure – without being noticed by the Philistines, who were lying in wait for him? How would the three thousand people who were on the temple roof, who came to see Samson humiliated, be able to see him? (The Septuagint changes the number to seven hundred; does this help?)

19. The Masoretes placed a hyphen between the word *nekam achat*, to assure that readers read verse 28 as "one revenge for my two eyes." However, Rashi, Radak, and others ignore the hyphen signifying "one revenge" and read the verse as saying, in the words of Rashi: "One [revenge for] one of the two [blinded] eyes, and a second reward [for the other blinded eye] hold for me for the world to come; but here give the reward for one of them" – the reward being the resumption of Samson's power so that he could kill the Philistines.

20. Others say it means "fish." Radak (on 1 Samuel 5:4) supposes that the idol had a form of a man from the waist up, while it was the likeness of a fish below the waist. Abarbanel thought

## HYPERBOLE

We have seen that the Bible uses exaggerations very frequently. Examples in this chapter are "all" of Samson's family members who came to secure his body for burial when we can assume that the family sent a delegation. Also it states that Samson judged "Israel," implying all twelve tribes, though we know the tribes were not united; he probably only served as a judge for his tribe Dan. The chapter states that about three thousand people were on the roof, gathered to watch the mocking of Samson; this should probably be understood as three groups of people since it is unlikely that so many people would stand on the roof.[21] Once we note the existence of hyperbole, we may want to consider that Samson was not as strong as the book portrays him and his feats were overstated.

---

Dagan looked like a fish from the waist up, but with hands and feet like a human, the opposite of Radak's view. These views are not based on any facts.

21. We would understand *eleph*, which could mean "thousand" or "units" in regard to the military, as "groups" here. Ehrlich imagines that Samson was made to perform first for the Philistines assembled below the roof with the idea that he would repeat his performance for the people on the roof later, but he killed the Philistines before the second performance.

## Excursus

# *Samson among the Rabbis*

*Maimonides wrote in his "Introduction to Perek Chelek" that people who accept rabbinical imaginative Midrashim as being true are fools and those who reject Midrashim entirely because they are not true are also fools. The proper approach to Midrashim is to realize that they are not true and were not meant to be taken as the truth, but to understand that the rabbis imparted these parables to teach lessons, and we should therefore mine the depth of the tales to see what they are teaching. With this caveat in mind, let us explore what the rabbis said about Samson.*

### TALMUDIC STATEMENTS CONCERNING SAMSON

The following is from the Babylonian Talmud, *Sota* 9. Virtually all of the imaginative ideas are not even implicit in the text.

1. Samson rebelled against God with his eye when he said in 14:3 that the Philistine woman was "pleasing in my eyes," so he was punished by the Philistines who put out his eyes in 16:21.
2. The beginning of Samson's degeneration happened in Gaza (16:1); therefore he was punished in Gaza (16:21).[1]
3. Delilah's name fit her (16:4). Playing on her name, the Talmud says the name implies that she weakened Samson's strength, heart, and actions.[2]

---

1. The Talmud notes that he had a prior amorous affair in Timnah, but says, "Nevertheless the start of his degeneration was in Gaza."
2. The rabbis frequently suppose that a name was given at birth because of some act that the person performed as an adult. This, of course, is impossible and should be understood as a homily.

4. During the fourth time that Samson told Delilah the source of his strength, Delilah realized that he was telling her the truth because, according to one rabbi's opinion, "words of truth are recognizable," and according to another rabbi's view, she heard Samson include God's name (in 16:17)[3] in his explanation and she knew that a pious man like Samson would never use God's name in vain.

5. Delilah "urged" Samson by detaching herself from him at the time of sexual consummation (16:16).

6. The angel's statement to "not eat any unclean thing" (13:4) means to not eat what Nazirites are forbidden to eat.

7. Samson lusted after that which is "unclean" (Philistine women), so when he was thirsty after killing many Philistines with an ass's jawbone, he drank water from an unclean thing, the jawbone (chapter 13).

8. Rabbi Chama ben Chamina interpreted "And the spirit of the Lord began" (13:25) as a reference to and fulfillment of Jacob's blessing (which the rabbi interpreted as a prophecy in Genesis 49:17): "Dan [meaning, a descendant of Dan] shall be a serpent in the way."

9. Although Genesis 21:23 states that there was a peace alliance between Abraham and the Philistines, Rabbi Chama ben Chamina explained that the alliance ended during the time of Samson.

10. Why did Samson use foxes when he placed torches on their tails to burn Philistine crops (15:4)? It was symbolic. When they are hunted, foxes run in a roundabout course; so too did the Philistines when they went back on the oath that the Philistine Abimelech had made to the patriarch Isaac. (This rabbi's view goes against the other rabbi's view, according to which the alliance had ceased.)

11. Rabbi Assi interpreted 13:25 as saying that Samson stood between two mountains, uprooted them, and ground them against each other.

12. Focusing on 13:24, Rav said Samson's physique was like that of other men, but his strength was like a fast-flowing stream (a hyperbole referring to his amorous passion).

---

3. God has no name. The "names" of God in Scripture are descriptions of God, reflecting that God is observable in the laws of nature that God created. The use of "name" here should be understood as "what people call God."

13. What did Samson pray when he sought strength to destroy the Dagan temple and the Philistines in it (16:28)? "God, remember the twenty years that I judged Israel when I never once ordered anyone to carry my staff from one place to another."

14. The width of Samson's shoulders was sixty cubits (about ninety feet) for he was able to carry the gates of Gaza on his shoulders, and there is a tradition that the gates were more than sixty cubits wide.

15. Verse 16:21 states that the Philistines forced Samson to "grind" in the prison house. This is a euphemism for sex. "Every man brought his wife to the prison so that she would bear a child by him" to have Samson's strength.

16. Rabbi Johanan said: "Samson judges Israel just as their father in heaven; as it [Genesis 49:16] reports, 'Dan [meaning Samson, who was from the tribe of Dan] shall judge his people as one'" (with one being understood as a reference to God).

It would be a mistake to suppose that one could look at these many Midrashim and find a common thread among them because each Midrash was developed by a different rabbi. Being human, each had a somewhat different view of the responsibilities of humans, and of what it means to be Jewish. However, we can see frequent use of hyperbole, treating events as allegories and details as symbols, a belief in punishment fitting the crime, the involvement of God in human events, and a lack of fear in discussing sex.

### DID ARCHEOLOGY DISCOVER SAMSON?

Archeologists found a stone seal that may prove that Samson is not a legendary figure, but a man who actually existed.[4]

The *Science Daily* of August 13, 2012, reported that archaeologists from Tel Aviv University discovered a circular stone seal in a house in Beth Shemesh, Israel; it is about 15 millimeters in diameter and it seems to depict a lion and a man.[5] The archeologists dated the stone to the twelfth century BCE, about the time that Samson may have lived. Professor Shlomo Bunimovitz, a codirector of the dig, reported that the seal helps "anchor the story [of Samson] in an archaeological setting."

---

4. My Wednesday morning study partner Dr. Jack Cohen brought this to my attention.

5. "Ancient seal may add substance to the legend of Samson," *Science Daily*, August 13, 2012.

The Israeli newspaper *Haaretz* reported the event on July 30, 2012, and stated that, "excavation directors Professor Shlomo Bunimovitz and Dr. Zvi Lederman of Tel Aviv University say they do not suggest that the human figure on the seal is the biblical Samson. Rather, the geographical proximity [of the stone seal] to the area where [the Bible states] Samson lived, and the time period of the seal, show that a story was being told at the time of a hero who fought a lion, and that the story eventually found its way into the biblical text and onto the seal."

# PART THREE

# CHAPTERS 17–21

# APPENDICES

*The final five chapters of Judges consist of what scholars call two appendices. The first appendix deals with the tribe of Dan (chapters 17 and 18) and the second one (18–21) with the tribe of Benjamin. They are called appendices because they do not mention any judges. Both refer to a Levite who is connected with Bethlehem (17:7 and 19:1), although each Levite was a different person. They tell of terrible events that occurred during the period of the judges, when apparently no judge judged, when there was "no king in Israel" (18:1 and 19:1), when "every man did what was right in his own eyes" (17:6 and 21:25).*

*Commentators on these five chapters differ as to when the events occurred. The general consensus, including Rashi and Gersonides, is that they describe episodes just after the death of Joshua and before the judgeship of the first judge Othniel.[1] They say the chapters were placed at the end of the book because they do not deal with judges, just occurrences that occurred during the period of the judges, and the horrendous stories of lawlessness serve as a good introduction to the book of Samuel and its story of the first Israelite king, Saul, which comes next in the Hebrew Bible. But others, such as Abarbanel and Radak, insist that the events in the five chapters occurred after the judgeship of Samson.*

---

1. One proof for the view that the events occurred at an early period is that chapter 18 tells how the tribe of Dan moved from the coastal region to the far north of Canaan, while in the story of Deborah in chapters 4 and 5, the tribe of Dan is already located in northern Canaan.

**Chapter 17**

# *Does Chapter 17 Mock the Kingdom of Israel?*[1]

*Chapter 17 introduces readers to Micah and his sanctuary. The nature of the golden image used in Micah's sanctuary has occasioned much discussion among scholars.*

MICAH'S SANCTUARY

Chapter 17 introduces us to Micah, a man from Ephraim. He stole a huge amount of money from his mother, who had promised the funds to God. After some time, Micah admitted the theft and returned the funds to his mother. She returned it to him to build a golden image and other objects for his home sanctuary. Micah used part of the funds to build these items, but pocketed the rest of the money that had been dedicated for God. Although the text does not describe the image that was constructed, some scholars state that it was a golden calf. Micah made his son the priest of his home sanctuary, but later, for unknown reasons, replaced him with a Levite for a stipulated annual sum.

Meanwhile, we read in chapter 18 that the tribe of Dan, driven from their land, was searching for a settlement and dispatched five spies to northern Canaan to reconnoiter the area. The spies happened to spend the night at Micah's estate, met the Levite priest, and saw the golden calf and other sanctuary articles.

They left in the morning and found an unprotected peaceful non-Israelite city in the north that was easy to conquer. They returned to their brethren and

1. A version of this chapter appeared in my book *A Rational Approach to Judaism and Bible Commentary*, published by Urim.

assembled a band of six hundred warriors to take the unprotected city from its unsuspecting inhabitants.[2]

The warriors passed Micah's estate and stole the golden calf and other property belonging to Micah. They sordidly persuaded the Levite priest to breach his contract with Micah and become the priest to their tribe when they conquered the undefended city. When Micah requested that they return his property, they threatened to kill him and his family if he continued to bother them, so he retreated. The warriors successfully conquered the peaceful city, killed its inhabitants, burned the city, rebuilt it, and named it after their tribe, Dan.

## THE USE OF CALVES IN ISRAELITE WORSHIP

The calf was first worshipped by the Israelites in the desert, after the exodus from Egypt (Exodus 32). Subsequently, it was worshipped for centuries by the Israelites in a later period. 1 Kings 12:26 ff tells the story of Jeroboam I of the kingdom of Israel, the nation that split off Judea after the death of King Solomon around 922 BCE. He erected two golden calves in the two temples he constructed in Beth-el and Dan. Some scholars state that he relied on the Israelite use of a calf in the exodus story, which seemed to indicate that calves have some sanctity. The calves were placed in the physically accessible courts of the temples where the people could touch them. It is uncertain whether the calves were meant to represent God or were seen as the seat or pedestal upon which the invisible God was thought to stand.

## MOCKING THE TEMPLES IN ISRAEL

Some scholars, but of course not all, offer an interesting interpretation of Judges 17 and 18 – the story of Micah's molten image. They contend that the story is "essentially negative, with marked ironical thrusts."[3] It was written in the southern kingdom of Judea to mock and reproach the temples of the northern kingdom of Israel, a polemic against the Dan sanctuary and its priesthood who claimed noble descent from the family of Moses.[4] The scholars claim that these two chapters

---

2. This was land in the extreme northern part of Canaan, land that Joshua did not divide among the tribes.

3. Soggin in his introductory commentary on chapter 17.

4. As seems to be indicated in 18:30.

were composed sometime after 722 BCE, when the temples at Beth-el and Dan were destroyed by invaders. The chapters, according to them, relate what they considered the repugnant origin of the golden calves that Jeroboam placed in his temples. The story in Judges shows that the golden calf at Dan existed for some time before Jeroboam and it came to Dan under disgraceful circumstances.[5] According to this perspective, the author of Judges 17 is implying that it was no wonder that the temple was destroyed around 722 BCE: it was punished for its despicable past.

PERSPECTIVES ON THE GOLDEN CALF IN EXODUS

Rashi justified the Israelite behavior regarding the golden calf by elaborating on a view mentioned in the Babylonian Talmud, *Shabbat* 89a, and *Midrash Exodus Rabba*. He suggested that the Israelites were misled by the demon Satan, who scared the people by causing a frightening turmoil in heaven and creating an anxiety-producing darkness. Satan told the people that Moses was dead, and proved it by showing them Moses's bier. The non-Israelite mixed multitude, who accompanied the Israelites during the exodus, were the first to succumb. They, in turn, enticed some, but not many, Israelites to join them. They threatened Aaron

---

5. Jeroboam led ten tribes and seceded from the empire of Kings David and Solomon around 926 or 922 BCE. He made himself king over the ten tribes and built two temples in Dan and Beth-el so that his people would worship there and not need to travel to the southern land of Judea from which they seceded.

The rabbis as well as the critical scholars differ about the calves installed by Jeroboam. Soggin, for example, states that Jeroboam's calves were not deities, but "the pedestal on which the God of Israel was raised, though this time invisibly, just as the ark in the Temple of Jerusalem was his throne." Kaufmann felt that Micah's temple was devoted to the Israelite God – there is no mention of Baal. Micah included four objects in his sanctuary – a *pesel, maseikha, ephod,* and *teraphim*. We do not know how they were used, but they were most likely fetishes rather than idols. Kaufmann adds that this was a time when there were many sanctuaries among the Israelites in Canaan, many of which were family temples.

According to 18:30, Moses's descendants served at the Dan temple "until the day of the captivity of the land," while 18:31 states "all the time that the house of God was in Shiloh" – a seeming contradiction. Rashi understands the two verses to refer to the exile of the ten northern tribes by Sennacherib, mentioned in II Kings 15:29. Radak suggests an earlier period, when the ark was taken by the Philistines from Shiloh (I Samuel 4:11); the Philistines probably destroyed the city at that point. Gersonides opts for a still earlier period: the exile of the Danites during the time of Jabin, king of Canaan, in Judges 4:2. And there are many other views, including that the two verses conflict and are two different traditions, both preserved by the editor of Judges.

with death. Aaron tried many tricks to delay them from carrying out their plan to substitute a calf for God. However, Satan harried the people. Aaron was assisted by magicians among the people, who produced the golden calf instantly though magic. This was Rashi's view in his commentary to Exodus 32.

Moses Maimonides passionately rebuffed such notions. He noted that a simple reading of the biblical text reveals that the people acted improperly. Unlike most other scholars, Maimonides stated in his *Guide of the Perplexed* 3:32 that God does not need the temple and its sacrificial services. However, God knew that humans required physical structures, prayers, and sacrifices, rather than intellectual thinking, which God preferred. Recognizing that humans can only change, grow and improve slowly, and preferring not to change human nature by miracles, God "allowed" the Temple services, sacrifices, and prayers. The immature, nonrational behavior of the Israelites with the golden calf was a paradigm of the lowest level of human nature, the need to express love to God by nonrational means, by using physical symbols.

## Chapter 18

# *The Shameful History of Micah's Temple*

*In the previous chapter, I discussed the notion that chapter 17 was composed to ridicule the temple that King Jeroboam built in Dan[1] because its history was "disgraceful." Yet it is uncertain whether this hypothesis is correct, because like much in the Bible, chapter 17 is filled with ambiguities and obscurities.*

FACTS TO CONSIDER

In evaluating the hypothesis that chapter 17 ridicules Jeroboam's temple, it is helpful to consider the following facts:

1. Chapter 17 seems to set the stage for a negative interpretation of Micah's behavior by first calling him by his full name Micahu, which means "who is like God," but later naming him Micah, without the ending signifying God, perhaps hinting at the ungodly circumstances of the story.[2]

2. Micah's initial behavior in his story is reprehensible and may indicate that we should judge all of his subsequent acts unfavorably. He steals eleven hundred shekels from his mother;[3] she, not knowing who has stolen her funds, responds by cursing the thief and promising the eleven hundred shekels to God if the money is returned.[4]

---

1. He built a second one in Beth-el.
2. Abarbanel ignores this hint and opines that Micahu was Micah's name when he was a child.
3. Micah and his mother form a contrast to Samson and his mother.
4. The sum of 1100 shekels is the exact amount of money the Philistines gave Delilah to seduce Samson into revealing the secret of his strength. Some scholars suggest that Micah's mother

3. Micah admits the theft and returns the money to his mother. She blesses him and gives the eleven hundred shekel back to him to build an image and other objects for his home sanctuary. Micah uses only two hundred shekels of the eleven hundred to build his sanctuary and sacred items and pockets the rest of the money that had been assigned for God's sanctuary. This was Micah's second theft.[5]

4. In chapter 18, we read that Micah's temple implements were stolen from him by the invading Danites to be used in their temple in their city Dan. The temple in Dan is now associated with three thefts.

5. Micah made his son the priest of his home sanctuary, but later, for un-known reasons, replaced him with a Levite, perhaps because the Levite was a professional. The Pentateuch states that only descendants of Aaron's family may function as priests and Levites may only aid priests. Scholars believe that during the early Israelite history, anyone, even a nonmember of Aaron's family or a Levite, could serve as a priest at an altar.[6] However, the author of chapter 17 may have considered the appointment of a son and Levite as a priest another improper act.[7]

6. This Levite seems to be described as an unsuccessful temple functionary who was itinerant and looking for any job he could pick up, and was for-tunate in finding a minor insignificant position as a family priest. He was unreliable. In chapter 18, although under contract with Micah, he aban-

---

was Delilah, but Rashi and Abarbanel reject this idea. I will discuss Abarbanel's unusual in-terpretation of parts of this story in the next chapter. Gersonides thought that by giving the blessing after she had cursed the thief, she was able to cancel the curse. This is unlikely. See the discussion in chapter 12 which describes how the ancients were convinced that once uttered, a vow, curse, or blessing could not be annulled. It should be recalled that Isaac also mistakenly gave his son Jacob a blessing he intended for his older son Esau. The effect of Isaac's blessing is the same as that of Micah's mother's curse. When Isaac realized his mistake, he said he could not cancel the blessing.

5. This is only one of several interpretations of a rather difficult text. Although there is no hint of it in the chapter, Rashi and Radak suppose that the passage means that Micah paid two hundred shekels as the worker's fee and nine hundred for the material. Martin writes: The payment of only part of the consecrated funds "may be [an additional] poking of fun."

6. II Samuel 8:18 states that King David's sons were priests, and they were not descendants of Aaron's family or Levites.

7. *Olam Hatanakh* offers a contrary view: the chapter is describing how the ancients worshipped God. Each family set an altar in their home and appointed one of their sons to minister in it.

dons him, joins the Danites for the prestigious position as tribal priest, and helps them build their temple in the north. Like Micah, he was part of the sordid history of the Dan temple.

7. Besides his sleazy behavior, Rashi writes that this man was only a Levite from his mother's side, but from the tribe of Judah on his father's side. Thus he wasn't really a Levite, for tribal affiliation descends from one's father. However, Ehrlich, Martin, Boling, and others suggest that the term *gar sham*, "lived there," in Judea, suggests that he was only a visitor to the tribe of Judah but not a tribal member. Rashi's disparagement also seems to conflict with an interpretation of 18:30 that states that he was "Jonathan, son of Gershom, son of Manasseh." The name Manasseh is spelt with a suspended letter *nun*. Radak quotes the rabbis in the Babylonian Talmud[8] who state that when the *nun* is not read, the name is Moses who brought the Israelites out of Egypt. The *nun* was added, although suspended above the name, to try to hide the embarrassing fact that this man who violated the Torah and led Israelites to worship idols was actually Moses's grandson.[9]

8. This chapter is also unclear about whether Micah's sanctuary was devoted to God or to an idol. The obscurity arises because the chapter uses the phrase "temple of God [*Elohim*]" and calls God by the divine name[10] *y-h-v-h*, but also states that Micah placed within it a *pesel*, which could denote a representation of God, an idol, a fetish, or even a golden calf. Rabbis and scholars differ as to whether Micah's temple was devoted to God or to an idol.[11] Those who see Micah doing wrong, interpret the tale as the building of a temple for an idol. They say that the *pesel*, the "molten image," set in the temple was a calf that was worshipped there, and refer readers

---

8. *Bava Batra* 109b–110a.

9. *Olam Hatanakh* suggests that the desire to protect Moses's honor also explains why 1 Chronicles 23:15–16 and 27:24 deleted Jonathan's name from the list of Moses's descendants. While it should be clear to us that only two generations after Moses are mentioned, there were obviously more than two, but it is characteristic of the Bible to indicate only the more important figures in lines of descent.

10. Actually, "name" in the Bible often means "essence." In relation to God, *y-h-v-h* denotes that God can be seen acting through the laws of nature.

11. Rashi, Targum Jonathan, and others suppose the temple was for idol worship. See Babylonian Talmud, *Shavuot* 35b.

to the calves that King Jeroboam set in his temples. They also note that Micah placed *teraphim* in his temple,[12] and while we no longer know what *teraphim* are, many people suppose they were "household idols."[13] Those, like Gersonides, who say Micah dedicated his temple to God refer to 17:13 where he says, "Now I know that *y-h-v-h* will show me favor, because I have a Levite as a priest." Soggin solves the problem by saying the temple had a syncretistic character, serving both the Israelite God and idols.

9. The Aramaic translation of Judges called Targum Jonathan also seems to treat Micah and his sanctuary in a mixed manner. When the five spies asked Micah's Levite priest to inquire of God whether they would be successful in 18:5, the translator treats their question as being directed to *y-h-v-h* and the Levite responded that *y-h-v-h* answered that they would succeed. Yet, the translator understands Micah's "house of God" in 17:5 to mean "house of idols," and in 8:24 – when Micah complains to the six hundred Danites, "You have taken my god" – as "idol." And whenever chapters 17 and 18 mention priest, the translator uses a word indicating a priest of idols. With this understanding of syncretism, an additional negative element is added to the history of the Dan temple: perhaps the originators intended to worship God, but their temple included idols and superstitious items such as the *teraphim* (which Rashi wrote were used for magic, and Gersonides said the magic did not work).[14]

10. The city of Laish[15] that the tribe of Dan captured and made their own was taken from "a people who were quiet and secure"[16] and "had no dealings

---

12. 17:5.

13. See Genesis 31:17–35 and I Samuel 19:13. In the former the *teraphim* were small, in the latter large. See also II Kings 23:24; Ezekiel 21:26; Hosea 3:4–5; and Zechariah 10:2. Gersonides supposed that they were not idols but items that people used to foretell the future, but he adds that despite the people's belief that the *teraphim* worked, they were unable to predict the future.

14. As previously stated, the chapter is filled with ambiguities. Radak, for example, understood that the Danites thought the *ephod* was used to communicate with God and did not know that it was used for idolatrous purposes.

15. In Joshua 19:47, Laish is called Leshem. The Bible often uses different names for the same place. In Genesis 14:14, the city is anachronistically called Dan even though it was not given this name until years after Moses's death. This too is characteristic. The Bible often calls a place by a name that it is not given until years later.

16. This passage contains another of many obscurities. It states that the people of Laish dwelt

with any man" (18:27–28). This describes a fourth robbery associated this time with murder – the Danites improperly seized the city from honest people who harmed no one, and killed them.[17] Martin writes: "This is the very antithesis of the heroic deeds of earlier figures in the book of Judges."

In short, this chapter shows Micah and those he encounters in a bad light, engaged in idol worship, theft, and murder. Since they are portrayed as being involved in one of the principle sanctuaries that King Jeroboam established, the chapter is stating in essence that the sanctuaries have a bad, even a foul foundation.

---

securely as the *tzidonim*. This word is obscure "either because of an error or because we no longer know the word's meaning" (*Olam Hatanakh*).

17. Cohen takes a different approach. He writes that the Danites burnt Laish because it was defiled by idolatry, to strike fear in the hearts of surviving inhabitants so they would not counterattack, and to terrorize the surrounding villages to stop them from seeking revenge.

**Excursus**

# Gersonides's and Abarbanel's Problematic Interpretations

*Both Gersonides and Abarbanel were highly intelligent people, but even very smart people can have ideas that others will consider irrational.*

## GERSONIDES

Levi ben Gershom, also known as Ralbag and as Gersonides (1288–1344), was born in Provence, France. He was a great philosopher and one of the most creative and daring minds of medieval Jewry. He was the author of a philosophical work called *The Wars of the Lord*, which his opponents sarcastically dubbed "The Wars against the Lord."

Like Saadiah, Abraham ibn Ezra, and Maimonides, Gersonides believed in the primacy of reason. In his *Wars*, he writes: "If the literal sense of the Torah differs from reason, it is necessary to interpret those passages in accordance with the demands of reason." He taught that a person is only obligated to accept the rabbinic interpretation of the Bible in respect to *halakha*, how the rabbis expected a Jew to behave, but not regarding their other statements. If the statement does not conform to reason, their statement must be interpreted in a way that conforms to reason.

He accepted much but not all of the philosophy of Maimonides. He agreed in his *Wars* that sacrifices are a concession and saw certain human, and not divine, values in the sacrificial service. Like ibn Ezra and Maimonides, he states that God is not involved in the daily governance of the world. Rather, the world functions according to natural laws. God does not know human individuals;

rather, he relates to the species of humanity. He does not take care of people; people must employ their intelligence and care for themselves. God does not communicate with people and prophecy is a higher level of intelligence. Since he, ibn Ezra, and Maimonides were persuaded that God is not involved in this world, it should come as no surprise that they agreed that God has no desire or need for sacrifices.

Gersonides, for example, was convinced that there was no miracle for Joshua making the sun stand still at Gibeon during Joshua's battle in Joshua 10. He suggested that Joshua was speaking figuratively; Joshua was saying that it was a wonder that he and his army were able to defeat the forces of five nations during such a short period, in a single day, while the sun was still shining.

In short, Gersonides believed much the same as ibn Ezra and Maimonides, although some variations in thought can be found. The most significant difference between the three rationalists is that, like most ancient people, Gersonides and ibn Ezra were convinced in the efficacy of astrology, while Maimonides considered it foolish and base idolatry.

Despite his general rationality, Gersonides also reflected the view of his age regarding women. The worst view of women that I ever read was by Gersonides, who wrote that women are mediocre creatures between animals and men. He listed more than a dozen lessons readers can learn from the Micah story and its aftermath – a story we will encounter in chapter 19; two reflect his view of women:

1. A woman should obey her husband, bear his misbehavior, and do what he wants. The Levite's concubine's failure to submit to her husband and her fleeing from him resulted in tens of thousands of deaths that we will be reading about, murders which would not have occurred if she had behaved properly.
2. When both a man and a woman are threatened with rape and one of the two must be surrendered, the woman should be handed over, as the Levite did his concubine.

## ABARBANEL

Don Isaac Abarbanel (1308–1437) wrote a detailed commentary of the Torah and generally preceded each chapter with very incisive questions, frequently delving into the psychology of divine and human behaviors, even though many of his solutions reflect a supernatural understanding of the Torah. For example, Abarbanel notes that God instructed Moses to have his brother Aaron perform the first three of the ten plagues because God knew that the Egyptian magicians would duplicate these plagues and did not want to embarrass Moses; once the magicians conceded defeat during the plague of lice, God transferred the actions to Moses.

Whereas Maimonides felt that having a king is a biblical mandate,[1] Abarbanel critiqued this view and many may feel that his view is more reasonable. If the Torah mandates rule by a king, he asked, why didn't Joshua appoint one and why did the prophet Samuel oppose monarchy? Abarbanel felt that the laws of monarchy in Deuteronomy 17:14–15 were like the laws involving the beautiful captive woman,[2] which the Torah disliked but permitted to avoid far less ideal behavior, as the Talmud notes: "The Torah states this in consideration of the evil inclination."[3]

However, Abarbanel had many ideas that would bother modern thinkers. He supposed, like Rashi, Nachmanides, and others, that God is involved in everything that occurs in this world and sometimes manipulates people, like puppets, to do the divine will. Even grass does not grow or rain fall unless God instructs it to do so. He imagined that God made Samson reveal that he was a Nazirite so that he would be weakened, captured, and tortured; and this would prompt Samson to take revenge against the Philistines for weakening and blinding him, and for their oppression of Israel. This latter view of God forcing a person to act is contrary to the view of rationalists such as Maimonides, who felt that people have free will and God does not manipulate people act as puppets.

When Scripture states that God hardened Pharaoh's heart, Maimonides ex-

---

1. *Mishneh Torah, Hilkhot Melakhim* 1:1–2. Maimonides accepted Rabbi Judah's opinion in the Babylonian Talmud, *Sanhedrin* 20b, even though other rabbis disagreed with Rabbi Judah. I am convinced that Maimonides recognized that virtually all, if not absolutely all, of the 613 "biblical commands" that he discusses in his *Sefer Hamitzvot* and *Mishneh Torah* are not biblical commands, but are command that the rabbis considered to be biblical. The distinction between what the rabbis considered "biblical" and those they mandated but did not consider biblical has certain consequences. I came to this conclusion by noting that Maimonides recognized in his *Guide of the Perplexed* that the rabbis changed many if not all of the biblical mandates (see *Guide of the Perplexed* 3:32) . Why didn't Maimonides say that these commands are ones that the rabbis considered biblical even though they are not mandated by the Bible, but only based on it? This would have confused the general population who felt that they were doing what God had commanded.
2. In Deuteronomy 21:10–14.
3. Babylonian Talmud, *Kiddushin* 21b.

plained that this was a natural occurrence, the result of the laws of nature God created: Pharaoh had repeatedly acted arrogantly against the Israelites until *his behavior* hardened his heart.[4]

Again, Abarbanel quarreled with Maimonides, who felt that humans cannot wrestle with angels and the story of Jacob wrestling with an angel must have been a dream. Abarbanel wrote that it could not have been a dream because Jacob limped after the encounter and one does not limp from a dream. My father Rabbi Dr. Nathan Drazin explained[5] that sometimes dreams are so traumatic that the effect of the dream stays, usually for only a short time, after the dreamer awakens. The Torah does not say that Jacob limped for a long time.

Abarbanel listed six lessons that people can learn from Micah's story in chapter 17. At least four of them are notions that most people today would find problematic.

1. One misdeed prompts others (*aveira goreret aveira*). Micah stole money from his mother in chapter 17, and the Danites stole his Levite and temple articles from him in chapter 18.

2. Most evils (*rov hara'ot*) come because of women. Adam sinned because of Eve and Micah sinned because his mother suggested that he build an idol.

3. When someone repents from an evil act (in Micah's case, stealing his mother's money), people should be careful not to suggest to him that he do another evil act, even something small, for once he has shown that he has a tendency to do wrong things there is a good chance he will do the small improper act and then advance to greater evils. Abarbanel understands that Micah's mother suggested that he make an idol with the money she gave him, he returned it to her saying he did not want to do so; she asked him again, and because he had developed a habit to do wrong in the past, he agreed to build the idol.

4. An oath made by a woman is worthless. Micah's mother vowed to donate to God the entire eleven hundred shekels that her son returned to her

---

4. Discussed in *Guide of the Perplexed* 2:48.
5. In a sermon to his congregation, Shaarei Tfilah, in Baltimore, Maryland.

after stealing her money, but she only contributed two hundred shekels to the project.

5. Men inherit their mother's nature. Micah made an idol on her suggestion and with her money, then improperly made his son the temple priest even though he was not a descendant of Aaron.

## Chapter 19

# *The Prelude to Civil War*

---

*Chapters 19–21 tell how members of the tribe of Benjamin committed egregious breaches of hospitality that led to civil war and the virtual destruction of Benjamin, and how after making a vow that could not be annulled the other tribes of Israel saved the tribe from extinction.*

---

### THE TERRIBLE STORY OF THE LEVITE'S CONCUBINE

In Judges 19 a Levite[1] living in the tribal area of Ephraim takes a concubine[2] from the tribe of Judah. She deserts him after having an adulterous affair with another man and goes to her father's house. Four months later,[3] he travels to his in-law's house to beg her to return to him. He had planned to stay only three days, but his father-in-law urges him three times on three successive days to stay longer. They leave late on the sixth day and have to stay overnight in the Benjamin city of Gibeah. A kind old man who was not a Benjamite, but a man from Ephraim who was sojourning in Gibeah, offers them shelter.[4]

Benjamite thugs, like those in Genesis 19, surround the old man's house and demand that he send out the Levite "that we may know him" (so we can sodomize him, Rashi). The old man refuses because of the basic law of hospitality. Like

---

1. This is a different Levite than the one in chapters 17 and 18. The two stories of Levites acting inappropriately show that during the period of the judges even Levites acted improperly (Abarbanel).
2. The judge Gideon had a concubine whose son was Abimelech. See 8:31. See also the Babylonian Talmud, *Sanhedrin* 21b, for the rabbinical views about concubines.
3. The same number of months is in 20:47.
4. Ironically, they avoided the closer city Jerusalem that was inhabited at the time by non-Israelites because they felt they would be safer with Israelites (Ehrlich).

Lot in Genesis 19, he offers his virgin daughter, and he also proposes giving them the Levite's concubine.[5] The Benjamites refuse. Nevertheless, the Levite pushes his concubine outside,[6] and the Benjamites "knew her, and abused her all night until morning, when they let her go." She crawls to the old man's house and dies on his threshold.

The Levite finds her in the morning when he was leaving.[7] He takes her body home, cuts it into twelve pieces, and sends the pieces throughout the land. Everyone who sees the pieces is outraged.

### BIBLICAL PARALLELS

The story in Judges 19 has many parallels. It is similar to the tale of the two angels visiting Abraham's nephew Lot in the city of Sodom in Genesis 19. The men of Sodom, as the men in Judges 19, wanted to sodomize the visitors, but they had no chance to do so to Abraham's angelic guests. The story of cutting up the dead concubine in Judges and sending the pieces to the twelve tribes in chapter 20 is somewhat analogous to what King Saul did when he cut up oxen and sent them throughout Israel to summon tribes to join him in battling Ammon; King Saul warned them that if they did not come he would cut them up as he had butchered the oxen.

### ARNOLD EHRLICH'S INTERPRETATION

Ehrlich states that the chapter is emphasizing that the protagonist is a Levite to inform readers that not only did the average Israelite act improperly during the period of the judges, but so did Levites who had the duty to serve in the temple and be an example to others.

In ancient times, once a daughter married, she was no longer under her father's control. In this chapter the concubine commits adultery, leaves her husband, and returns to her father's house; but her father has no control over her because she had married. The chapter relates that the concubine met her husband and took

---

5. Why didn't the law of hospitality apply to the concubine? Was it because she was a woman?

6. This "was a dastardly act to save himself" (Cohen).

7. It is unclear if the Levite meant to leave town without recovering his concubine because she was damaged goods and had been defiled by other men.

him to her house. It was her decision – not her father's – to reconcile and return with him.

Yet, while she is a central figure in the drama, she does not speak in the chapter. Is this a reflection of discrimination against women? Ehrlich notes later that the husband and his father-in-law sat and dined, but the concubine was not present at the meal because men and women did not eat together in these ancient days.

Her father is overjoyed at the reconciliation because his daughter had committed adultery, and it was therefore unlikely that another man would want her. Now he wouldn't have to support her.

We are told that the husband slept in his father-in-law's house for three days.[8] This suggests euphemistically that he slept with his concubine, and that her father knew it and was now certain that a reconciliation had occurred. The father was so happy that he kept encouraging his son-in-law to stay longer. He did so three times, and the pair left late on the sixth day after the husband's arrival.

Sometimes an unintentional result occurs from an intended good deed. The father-in-law begged his son-in-law to remain three times. He listens to him and even leaves late on the sixth day because his father-in-law suggested that they have a final meal together. The trip would normally take a single day, but since the pair left late on the sixth day, they had to stay overnight in the Benjamite town Gibeah, with dire consequences.

The chapter mentions three times (verses 3, 10, and 19) that the Levite had many supplies with him to show that despite being wealthy, the evil Benjamites treated him badly. Similarly, although stated in verse 9 that the Levite's concubine was with him, this fact is repeated in verse 10 to show why the Levite felt he needed to stay in a fortified town, to protect his concubine. "This is characteristic; the Bible explains matters such as these by repetitions. It doesn't do so with many

---

8. The use of three occurs several times in this chapter: the number of days the Levite intended to stay with his father-in-law, the three times his father-in-law begged him to delay his departure, the three times the chapter mentions the Levite's provisions, and the three uses of *vayachazeik*, "retained" and "took hold": in verse 4 the father-in-law hospitably restrained the Levite; in 25 the Levite took hold of his concubine and pushed her out to the rabble; and in 29 he took hold of her dead body and severed it into twelve pieces. It is ironically first used in a positive sense but later in a vicious manner.

words of explanation as do nonbiblical writings. Remember this, don't forget it, for this will open your eyes [in understanding] Holy Scripture."[9]

Scholars are bothered by the text indicating that the Levite told the old man, "I am now going to the house of the Lord" (verse 18) since it is clear that he had no intention of going there; he was going home. Many interpretations are given. Ehrlich suggests that this is an error; the original text was *v'et y-h-v-h ani holeikh*. The Levite was assuring the old man that despite so many Israelites worshipping idols, "I follow God." (Although Ehrlich does not mention it, this is another ironic statement. The Levite did many improper acts with his concubine.)

When the old man offered his virgin daughter and the Levite's concubine, the Benjamites refused to listen. They rejected his offer because they did not want to harm the old man, a fellow townsman, only his visitors.

## A RADICAL VIEW CONSISTENT WITH PAST UNDERSTANDINGS

"All Israel" respond to the Levite's call for revenge. They demand the surrender of the perpetrators of the concubine's rape and murder. When the tribe of Benjamin refuses, they wage war against the tribe and virtually decimate it.

> It is likely that the term "all Israel" is a typical biblical overstatement. We noticed in the past that Scripture uses the descriptive term "all" when it means "many," but not "every." For example, the Bible says frequently that Moses spoke to all of Israel, which he could not have done without a microphone, so it must mean that he spoke to many Israelites, perhaps just tribal leaders.
>
> We see that this chapter mentions two tribes frequently. The Levite and the old man who helps him are from Ephraim. The villains in the episode are Benjamites. We saw previously that the tribe of Ephraim acted in a hostile manner and attempted to assume a leadership role in chapters 8 and 12.[10]

This narrative is most likely describing a war between Ephraim and Benjamin, the third time in Judges that the people of Ephraim are forcibly asserting what they think is right. Alternatively, if other tribes were involved, it is possible that they joined to aid Ephraim and acted under its leadership.

---

9. My translation of Ehrlich.

10. The tribe of Judah is mentioned as the home of the Levite's father-in-law, the man who treated the Levite hospitably.

This interpretation raises the question: Is the author of Judges portraying Ephraim, the tribe of King Jeroboam who seceded from Judah and established his own kingdom in Israel, in a negative fashion, similar to what I discussed in chapter 17? As we will see, the attack against Benjamin was despicable and foolhardy, and the attackers themselves realized they did wrong. Did the author contrast the foolishness of Ephraim and the cruelty of some Benjamites with the proper behavior and peaceful nature of Judea, as shown by the behavior of the Levite's father-in-law, who lived in Judah?[11]

### OTHER COMMENTARIES

Some rabbis attempted to soften the tale. Rashi states that the concubine did not commit adultery; the root z-n-h in verse 2 does mean adultery, but it could also be explained as she "departed."[12] Targum Jonathan, from whom Rashi derived his interpretation, changed "committed adultery" to "despised," thereby giving the reason for her departure. The Septuagint translation, Boling, Soggin, and others state she was "angry." Most of these commentators see the fault of the marital crisis lying with the husband, but it was not serious because we see that the wife and father-in-law were glad to be reconciled.[13]

Radak writes that the concept of adultery also exists with a concubine because in those days a concubine was a wife without a *ketuba*, a marriage contract designed to protect wives. In a *ketuba* a husband promises to pay his wife a stipulated sum in the event of divorce. This interpretation cannot be true because the institution of the *ketuba* originated many centuries after this event in Judges. Gersonides imagines that the concubine couldn't have committed adultery because Deuteronomy 24:4 forbids a husband to retake his wife after she had sex with another man.[14]

---

11. If this conjecture is correct, the taking of the concubine from Judah could be seen as symbolic of Jeroboam taking the ten tribes from the Judean nation of King David's descendant and forming his own nation, Israel.

12. It is used often to refer to Israelites who depart from God.

13. Soggin notes that this is the only instance in the Hebrew Bible where the woman separates, because in the Bible it is only the man who has the right to repudiate his wife. However, he informs readers that women have this right in the Code of Hammurabi (art. 142). Soggin apparently ignored the incident of Abraham's concubine leaving him when she felt persecuted by Sarah.

14. His view is based on the Babylonian Talmud, *Gittin* 6b.

Ignoring the issue of the *ketuba*, Martin notes that a "concubine had a legal marital status, as is shown by the fact that the man is referred to as her 'husband' in verse 3. In addition, the concubine's father is called the Levite's 'father-in-law' in verse 4, and the Levite is referred to as his 'son-in-law' in verse 5."

Targum Jonathan moderates the Benjamite treatment of the concubine in verse 25 to "they knew her and ridiculed her the entire night."

Our Hebrew text has the Levite sending the twelve pieces of the concubine throughout all of Israel without mentioning any message. The Septuagint translation adds to verse 30 and switches around the order; in this reading, the Levite told the men he sent with the pieces to say to every Israelite, "Has anything like this ever been seen? Consider it and speak your minds." So everyone who saw the pieces said, "No such thing ever happened or was seen before."

Abarbanel understood that the Benjamite rabble were not interested in homosexual sex with the Levite.[15] This explains why the old man and the Levite did not offer the Levite's male servant. The rabble wanted the concubine because they saw that she was beautiful. The Levite understood this and sent her out to them. Abarbanel also imagined that the Levite sent pieces of his concubine also to Benjamin since all Benjamites were not involved in her rape and murder; he did not know that they would side with and support the evil men of Gibeah.

---

15. Gersonides has the same view. He adds that they must have always wanted her because if they were only interested in homosexuality, why did they continually rape her when they had her in their possession.

# Chapter 20

# *Another Civil War*

---

*Chapter 20 describes another Israelite civil war: all of Israel against the tribe of Benjamin. However, if our supposition mentioned in the last chapter is correct, it is the tribe of Ephraim alone or as the leader of a coalition that is fighting against the tribe of Benjamin.[1]*

---

## THE PREVIOUS CIVIL WAR

This is not the first time that Ephraim is involved in civil war. In chapter 11 Ephraim complained to Jephthah that he failed to call them to be part of the battle against Ammon, probably because they wanted a share of the spoils. This complaint to Jephthah was their second protest; the first was their similar grievance against Gideon.[2] Unlike Gideon, Jephthah did not appease Ephraim with words, but instead started a brutal civil battle resulting in many deaths. Just as Jephthah's civil war was unnecessary, cruel, and immoral, so too was Israel's war against

---

1. We saw in the past that there is some support for the idea that the book of Judges was composed to highlight the importance of the tribe of Judah, with its Davidic dynasty, and to belittle Ephraim. In chapter 1 and in this chapter, God tells the Israelites that the tribe of Judah should lead them in battle. In this chapter the combat is against Benjamin. King David's predecessor as king over Israel was Saul of Benjamin. When David became king of Israel there were still people who felt that the family of Saul should rule. It is possible, although there is no proof, that this chapter is disparaging Saul's tribe. Benjamin was not a peaceful tribe. Jacob called it a "ravenous wolf; in the morning he devours prey, and in the evening he divides spoil" (Genesis 49:27). The tribe went to war in Judges 3 in the days of judge Ehud and joined judge Deborah in Judges 5.

Although Ephraim may have been the instigator or leader of the civil war, the chapter states that God said Judah should be in the front line.

2. In chapter 8.

Benjamin, and the Israelites realized this after they butchered tens of thousands of their brethren.

### THE CIVIL WAR AGAINST BENJAMIN

In chapter 20, all[3] of the Israelites had gone up "to the Lord at Mizpah"[4] to hear the Levite tell how the Benjamites of Gibeah killed his concubine. Among the Levite's claims, he states that the Benjamite rogues intended to kill him.[5] An army of 400,000 enraged Israelite soldiers[6] sends messages throughout the Benjamin territory demanding that the tribe turn over the culprits.[7] Benjamin refuses. "They flocked from their town to Gibeah to engage in war with the Israelites." They muster 26,700 men.[8] The Israelite soldiers draw lots to select a tenth of their force, to secure provisions for the fighters.

---

3. There are many exaggerated statements in this chapter. As usual, the Bible's "all" means "many."
4. Why did they assemble at Mizpah? The chapter does not say. The use of "to the Lord" seems to indicate that, contrary to the traditional belief that there was only a single sanctuary and it was at Shiloh, there was a sanctuary in Mizpah as well and at Beth-el (Ehrlich). It is also possible that Mizpah was a place of assembly for the tribes: Saul was crowned in the city in 1 Samuel 10:17 ff. Beth-el, in contrast, was the city where the Israelites went to obtain an oracle from God.
5. The intent to kill the Levite is not mentioned in chapter 19, which only indicates that they wanted to "know him." Among other possible explanations for its absence: (1) The Levite may have exaggerated his plight to enrage the Israelites. (2) The claim may be true. Scripture very frequently states something briefly and then elaborates upon it later, adding details when the event is retold. We will see another example of this writing style in the description of the battles.
6. Scholars consider the numbers in this chapter to be exaggerations. Soggin and others note that the Israelites went "with arms already in its hands, i.e. in such a way as almost to invite the tribe in question, well known for its pride and arrogance, *not* to hand them over.... Benjamin virtually had to refuse."
7. Abarbanel focuses anachronistically on later Jewish law and asks what the legal basis for killing the malefactors is. Among other suppositions, he suggests that if the concubine was considered a wife, the Benjamites committed adultery with her with the punishment being death. If she was not a wife, the "conditions of the time" required it. See chapter 4 for a discussion of this rabbinical law.
8. The verses state that 25,000 Benjamites were killed in the final battle and 600 escaped. This leaves 1,100 unaccounted for. Although not explicit, Radak states that about a thousand were killed in the first two of the three battles and the one hundred is not stated in the 25,000, even though the true count of the dead Benjamites in the third battle was 25,100 because Scripture frequently rounds off numbers. There is a Midrash that printers placed in parenthesis in Rashi – perhaps believing that Rashi did not include it in his writing – that the hundred escaped to Rome.

The Israelites travel to Beth-el[9] and inquire of God, "'Who should go first for us to battle Benjamin?' And the Lord said, 'Judah first.'" The Israelites suffer a huge defeat in this first battle: twenty-two thousand deaths. The Israelites return to Beth-el and weep. "They asked the Lord, 'Should I go again to battle Benjamin, my brother?'[10] And the Lord said, 'Go up against him.'" The Israelites did so and lose again; this time eighteen thousand men.[11] They petition God a third time,[12] asking, "Should I go again to battle Benjamin my brother, or should I cease?" God answers, "Go up, for tomorrow I will deliver him into your hand."

In this third clash the Israelite troop used Joshua's ambush tactic, described in Joshua 8, in his combat against the city of Ai: they drew the Benjamites from their city by means of a feigned flight.[13] They were so successful that only six hundred Benjamin men survived, by dint of running away and hiding. The Israelites killed not only more than twenty-six thousand Benjamite warriors but

9. Beth-el was a sacred place during the days of the patriarchs (Genesis 28:10–22 and 35:1–7). Jeroboam built his temple there, as well as in Dan (1 Kings 12:31–33 and Amos 7:13). If Gibeah had a sanctuary, as I stated previously, why did the Israelites leave this sanctuary and go to the one at Beth-el? The chapter tells us this was because the ark was there at that time. We do not know how the Israelites made their three inquiries of God. Kaufmann writes that there is no mention in the Bible of seeking God's advice through a priest, so this was not the reason for assembling at Beth-el. He also notes that there is no mention here that there was, as in the days of Moses, an Ohel Moed. Perhaps the ark was used in some fashion, such as speaking in front of it. Some rabbis in the Babylonian Talmud (*Yoma* 73b), Gersonides, Elitzur, and others say they did so through the Urim, but the Urim is not mentioned in Judges.

10. This time, they added "my brother."

11. The Babylonian Talmud, *Sanhedrin* 103b, and Rashi state the forty thousand Israelite soldiers died because the Israelites failed to stop Micah from building a sanctuary to an idol. The rabbis holding this view felt that the community as a whole is guilty for not stopping "sin." Another rabbinical explanation is that God was not pleased with the Israelites fighting a civil war and punished them by allowing forty thousand deaths. Another idea is that God did not cause the deaths, but simply avoided helping the Israelites until the third attempt. Still another, by Gersonides and Ehrlich, is that God was not satisfied with their query until they added the third time "or should I cease." The first queries, according to this view, were arrogant; they reflected the Israelites' determination to go to war and unwillingness to be told otherwise by God.

12. As usual, the number three reappears frequently. It is also part of the third-day ambush tactic. A small group attacked the city and pretended to flee in panic. A second group lay hidden, prepared to attack the city when the Benjamites left it to chase the first group. A third element waited until the Benjamites left the city and attacked them.

13. The fact that the Israelites used the Joshua tactic and did not rely on God to secure their victory lends support to the interpretation that the civil war was a natural event and God was not involved.

every Benjamite woman, child, and animal. I will discuss this "immoral practice" in the next chapter.

## INTERPRETATIONS BY EHRLICH

The following are Arnold Ehrlich's interpretations to chapter 21:

1. The tenth of the Israelite forces – forty thousand of the four hundred thousand – assigned to procure provisions for the battle were chosen by lots.[14] Since the men in this logistic unit did not have to engage in battle, many men preferred this safe assignment, and the fairest way to determine its participants was by lots.

2. Out of all the Israelite conflicts mentioned in Scripture, why is this the only one that required a logistic unit? When the Israelites fought in their homeland, the soldiers brought their own food or their families brought it to them, as David's father sent David with food for his brothers who were in King Saul's army.[15] When the Israelites fought outside their homeland, they lived off the produce of the enemy land. Here, the Israelites did not want to take food from the Benjamites, just as they took no spoil after defeating them, so that it would be clear to all that they did not fight their brother tribe to obtain spoils or even food. (Ehrlich may be right, but there is a frequently used biblical style of not stating everything – certainly not the obvious, such as providing food and other supplies. A slight variation to Ehrlich's question and answer is: Why does this book tell readers about the logistical unit when Scripture does not do so elsewhere in describing other wars? The answer: to emphasize that the Israelites did not want anyone to think they battled a brother tribe to secure wealth.)

3. Why did God tell the Israelites to fight Benjamin twice when God must have known they would be defeated in these confrontations? God opposed the notion that the act of some men in raping the concubine gave the other tribes the right to engage in civil war and the murder of thousands of people. The Israelites should have sent messengers to the elders

---

14. Lots are mentioned in verse 9.
15. 1 Samuel 17:17. This was when David asked Saul for permission to fight the Philistine giant Goliath.

of Benjamin requesting the deliverance of the alleged culprits for trial. Instead the Israelites sent messengers throughout all of Benjamin telling the Benjamites about the atrocity. This was improper. Their behavior suggested that they were seeking an excuse to wage war against the entire tribe. (If we believe God was not involved in the affair at all, we would understand that the inquiry was part of the normal war planning of Israel's leaders: "Should we fight Benjamin, and if so, how?" Their tactics failed twice until they used the ambush technique.)

4. The mention of Pinchas in verse 28, a third generation after Moses (he was Moses's brother Aaron's grandson), supports the view that Judges 17–21 occurred just after the death of Joshua, before the onset of the period of the judges. This dating is also supported by the book's statement that at the time there was no king in Israel.[16] The phrase "no king" means no leader, not even a judge.

## ARE THERE TWO DIFFERENT TALES OF THE CIVIL WAR IN THIS CHAPTER?

Some scholars think there are two different descriptions of battles in this chapter. They suppose that the book's editor had both versions and rather than deciding which to place in his book, he put both of them, despite them having different details. These scholars failed to take account of a frequently used biblical writing style, which we encountered in the past. Biblical writers often state an event briefly and then follow it with details. Thus verses 11–13, 23–25, and 36–46 are not different versions of what precede it, but the details of the prior general statement.

## DID THE PATRIARCH JACOB FORETELL EVENTS?

People could read statements in Genesis 49 as foretelling what occurred during the days of the judges as well as afterwards.

In Judges 1:29, we read how Ephraim was unsuccessful in driving out Canaanites from the land they wanted to conquer. We can suppose that this must have depressed the tribe, and when they saw an opportunity they would want to express their superiority over the other tribes. We saw two clear instances, regarding Gideon and Jephthah, as well as possibly in the leadership of the civil

---

16. 18:1, 19:1, and 21:25.

war in this chapter, where Ephraim seemed to show that they felt they were the leadership tribe.

Ephraim had a claim to this lofty position since Ephraim and Manasseh were the children of Joseph, who was both the oldest son of Jacob's beloved wife Rachel and Jacob's favorite child. Jacob gave Joseph a double portion, which was traditionally handed to firstborn children, showing that he considered Joseph his firstborn son. In Genesis 48:13, Jacob placed his right hand on Joseph's younger son Ephraim indicating that he would be the more significant child.

In Genesis 49:23–24, Jacob predicts about Joseph: "The archers have dealt bitterly with him, and shot at him, and hated him, but his bow abode firm." In 49:25, Jacob predicts that God will bless Joseph. People who enjoy reading biblical foretelling into scriptural verses could find the first quote referring to three events: the two civil wars, and Jeroboam's secession from the Davidic dynasty and establishment of a kingdom in the north that he called Israel.

Judah is pictured in Genesis 49 as successful in war and the ruler of the tribes. This military and leadership role can be seen in Judges 1 and 20, where God tells the tribes that Judah should lead them in battle. Thus, the ambiguity regarding the leadership over Israel in Genesis 49 – is Judah or Joseph to lead? – is a tension that persisted for centuries.

Chapter 49 also describes Benjamin in what could be said to reflect the tribe's behavior in Judges 20: "Benjamin is a ravenous wolf. In the morning he devours prey, and in the evening he divides spoil."[17]

---

17. Genesis 49:27. While Genesis seems to reflect the view that Ephraim is a superior tribe, Numbers and Deuteronomy do not. The division of Joseph into two tribes, giving prominence to Ephraim, is overlooked in Deuteronomy 27:11–13 and is minimized in Deuteronomy 33:13–17. In Numbers 34:17–29, the tribe of Judah tops the tribal list and it was Judah, not Ephraim, that led the tribal march throughout the forty years in the desert.

**Excursus**

# Why Women and Children Are Killed in the Bible

*Many people prefer to believe that every event and law mentioned in the Bible is true, perfect, and reflective of the highest level of morality, since Scripture is divine. Maimonides taught the opposite: The Torah had to deal with the primitive mindset of the people when Scripture was given to them. Therefore, the Torah contains many laws and descriptions of behavior that fit the ancient period and its worldview, which are far from ideal. Three of the many nonideal behaviors are sacrifices, the command to murder rebellious children, and the practice of killing every inhabitant of a condemned captured town, including women and children.*

## THE ANCIENT ISRAELITE MINDSET

Historians, social scientists, and thinkers such as Maimonides recognized that the early Israelites existed in a hostile world filled with superstitions, absorbed the primitive notions of the surrounding people, and suffered prolonged periods of educational neglect because of centuries of enslavement, desert wanderings, and constant battles after they entered and conquered Canaan.

Maimonides felt that the early generations were not only intellectually, scientifically, and morally inferior, but they had undeveloped ideas about God and what was required of them and society. He wrote in his *Guide of the Perplexed* 3:32 that the Israelites accepted "the customs that existed in those days generally among all men, and the mode of worship in which the Israelites were brought up."

The Torah recognized, Maimonides wrote, that it was impossible to wean the people suddenly from ancient heathen notions. "It was in accordance with the wisdom and plan of God...that God did not command us to give up and discontinue all these kinds of (behaviors and worship) service, for to obey such a commandment would have been contrary to human nature, for people generally cleave to that to which they are accustomed." But the Torah modified the ancient behaviors somewhat and showed that they should be modified further. In 3:51, Maimonides states that people will ultimately improve and come to understand true worship and proper behavior. Thus, it should surprise no one that there are remnants of many pagan practices in the Bible and that the rabbis attempted to change, elevate, sublimate, and rationalize them.

SACRIFICES

Maimonides states in 3:32 that the primitive mindset of the early Israelites prompt-ed the Torah to "allow" sacrifices. This concession was made only because the Israelites were so accustomed to sacrifices that it would have been psychologically impossible to wean them away from sacrifices at the early stage of their develop-ment as a nation.

The fact that sacrifices are mentioned in the Torah does not suggest that the Torah approved of them. Maimonides wrote in 3:32 that God opposed sacrifices, and the prophets expressed God's opposition. According to Maimonides, the prophets frequently rebuked "their fellow men for being over-zealous and exert-ing themselves too much in bringing sacrifices. The prophets distinctly declared that the object of the sacrifice is not very essential, and that God does not require sacrifices."

Many people think that the Torah's elaborate laws concerning sacrifices show its pleasure in the sacrificial system. Maimonides explains that the opposite is true: many details are given to help wean the people from the practice. Laws restricted the sacrifices: they allowed only some kinds of animals to be sacrificed and only in certain times and places. The Torah even instituted "purity" laws whose goal was to minimize the attendance of people in the sanctuary.

The rabbis understood that sacrifices were only a concession to the primitive nature of unsophisticated humanity. When the temple was destroyed in 70 CE, many Jews felt, as did the Samaritans, that sacrifices could continue outside the temple just as had been the custom in earlier Israelite history. But the rabbis saw this as a good time to stop the practice. They replaced it with a higher level of devotion to God: study and prayer.

### MURDERING REBELLIOUS CHILDREN

Deuteronomy 21:18–21 is another example of a primitive practice that the Torah wanted to change. It contains the law of the *"ben sorer u'moreh,"* the stubborn and rebellious son: "If a man has a stubborn and rebellious son, that will not hearken to the voice of his father, or the voice of his mother, and though they chasten him, will not hearken unto them; then his father and mother should lay hold of him, and bring him out unto the elders of the city, and unto the gate of his place, and they shall say unto the elders of the city: 'This our son is stubborn and rebellious, he doth not hearken to our voice; he is a glutton, and a drunkard.' And all the men of the city shall stone him with stones that he dies; so shall thou put away the evil from the midst of thee; and all Israel shall hear and fear."[1]

This law reflected the practice of the ancient brutal paternalistic society of the time, in which a father had supreme control over his wife and children and could kill his child if he wanted to do so. The Torah mitigated the practice somewhat, in a manner that the ancient Israelites could accept, although it is still too harsh by modern standards. For example, the Torah removed total control from the father; he had to bring the case to the elders (a court) for an objective decision. He must bring his wife, whose views were listened to. Parents had to warn the child to behave. A father was not allowed to kill his son; this was done by the community which, presumably, did not kill children without some thought. Yet, children grow, mature, and change; gluttony and drunkenness are not grounds for capital punishment, and people should not be killed for what may happen to them in the future.

Thus, like many other biblical practices, the rabbis stated that this law should no longer be implemented. The Talmud[2] read into the passage a multitude of preconditions that made capital punishment impossible. Among much else, they said the law only applied if the boy's father and mother were physically identical in appearance and stature and in the tones of their voices, which was impossible.

---

1. The Jewish Publication Society translation.
2. Babylonian Talmud, *Sanhedrin* 71a.

The Talmud asks: If as we now understand the law, it is impossible to implement, "Why then was the law written?" It answers: "That you may study it and receive reward." The Talmud contends that this law was never implemented in the past, but includes a report of a sage who stated that he saw the grave of such a son. How should we understand these talmudic statements?

The first – "study it and receive a reward" – denotes, to my mind, that we should study and realize that the rabbis understood that the Torah law was an improvement over the practices of the time, but it needed further improvement; and the improvement should be in the enlightened spirit of the Torah. Once this development of the law is understood, further growth can be implemented and individuals and society will be rewarded.

The second – the conflict between the statement that the law was never implemented and the testimony that it was implemented – suggests that although it is true that such a disobedient son was killed in the past, we should behave as if it never happened: we should understand that the Torah is teaching that such an act should never have been done.

### KILLING ALL INHABITANTS OF A CONQUERED CITY

Biblical and rabbinic sensitivity and commitment to people's improvement are also seen in the law of a conquered city. Ancients, including the Israelites, were convinced that when a city contains evil people, these people pollute the city, and the city and all in it must be destroyed, including women, children, and animals. This is because (1) otherwise the evil pollution will spread, (2) the ancients believed that the group is responsible for the wrongs of individuals, and (3) the people who aren't evil are still guilty because they should have rid/cleansed the city of its evil.

But this law was modified. Deuteronomy 20:16–18 states concerning the conquest of Canaan: "The cities of these people that the Lord your God is giving you as an inheritance – you must save nothing that breathes. You must utterly destroy them…so they do not teach you to do their abominations."

Many rabbis noted the ethical dilemma of harshly slaying innocent people and proposed a reading of Deuteronomy that required the Israelites to submit peace offers to the Canaanites. The Talmud,[3] for example, contends that Joshua was

---

3. Jerusalem Talmud, *Sheviit* 10:5, 16:2. The three offers were: if you are willing to make peace,

told by Moses to propose peace, and Joshua sent three letters to the Canaanites before entering their country offering peace. The Bible explicitly states that Moses himself offered peace to Sihon king of Heshbon (Deuteronomy 2:26).

This law to kill all Canaanites was never implemented. Even a cursory reading of the books of Joshua and Judges show that the Israelites lived among the Canaanites. This is another of many examples where the Torah and rabbis began the amelioration of biblical commands.

### THE CONDEMNED CITY

Deuteronomy 13:13–19 contains the law of the condemned city: If the Israelites hear that in one of their cities base fellows enticed citizens to worship "other gods," they must "inquire, search, and look diligently." If they find that the allegations are true, "you must smite all the city inhabitants with a sword, destroying it utterly, everything in it, even cattle." No spoils may be taken; "they must be burned."

This, like the biblical laws of sacrifices, the rebellious son, and the conquest of Canaan, was a step above the practices of surrounding nations. A three-fold inquiry was necessary, and over-enthusiastic and badly motivated acts were controlled by the rule forbidding the taking of spoil.

As with the law of the son, the rabbis read rules into the biblical mandate that made the practice impossible.[4] They said if the city contained a single mezuzah or if a camel driver passed through the city, the destruction could not take place. The rabbis added, as they did about the son, that the law was never implemented – it was taught in order that we study and get rewarded – yet rabbis saw ruins where it had been implemented in the past. These statements should be understood as I explained previously.

### ANOTHER EXAMPLE OF RABBINICAL SENSITIVITY

The Torah (Exodus 2:11–17) describes three events in which Moses saved people, thereby showing readers that they too must be sensitive to people. The rabbis added a fourth event.

---

we are also willing; if you want to leave Canaan, we will let you leave (the Gigashites left); if you want war, make war.

4. Babylonian Talmud, *Sanhedrin* 71a and 111b–113b.

After Moses grew up in the Egyptian palace, he "went out to his brothers" and saw an Egyptian hitting a Hebrew. He killed the Egyptian and saved the Hebrew.

Later, he saw two Hebrews fighting and interfered to stop the two Hebrews from hurting each other. When one said to Moses, "Do you want to kill me as you killed the Egyptian?" Moses realized that his murder of the Egyptian was known and he escaped to Midian.

In Midian, he saw shepherds driving seven women shepherds from a well. He aided the women and helped them water their flock.

In these three episodes Moses aided the weak in different ways: (1) when a Hebrew was harmed by a non-Hebrew, (2) when two Hebrews fought with each other, and (3) in a conflict between non-Hebrews. The Torah teaches that people should aid others no matter who they are.

The rabbis imagined a fourth instance. Moses was pasturing a flock in Midian when one animal was lost. He went in search of the animal and saved it. God said: "This man who showed concern for a flock of animals is the man I need to care for my flock, Israel."[5]

In essence, the rabbis extended the concept of compassion from humans to animals.

---

5. J.H. Hertz, ed., *The Pentateuch and Haftorahs* (Soncino, 1960), page 213.

## Chapter 21

# *More Rapes and a Third Civil War*

The author or authors of Judges emphasize the Israelite depravity four times[1] in the final five chapters by stating, "In those days there was no king in Israel; each man did what he felt was right." Chapter 17 tells about a man stealing from his mother and from the sanctuary and building a house for an idol. The "holy" items in this house as well as its priest are stolen from him in chapter 18 by Danites who destroy the inhabitants of a peaceful Canaanite city in order to settle the area for themselves. They establish a temple there that will serve for many years as a site for idol worship. In chapter 19, rogue inhabitants of a Benjamite town rape a concubine and her husband callously cuts up the woman and sends the pieces throughout Canaan to incite Israelites against the killers. The Israelites decide to engage in a civil war against the entire tribe of Benjamin because of the deed of some criminals in a single city. This was the second civil war in this book. The first, also unnecessary, was led by Jephthah who could have appeased Ephraim as his predecessor Gideon did under the same circumstances.[2] Chapter 20 tells about the war against Benjamin, the death of over forty thousand Israelites, and the near destruction of the tribe of Benjamin.

### FINDING WIVES FOR THE BENJAMITES

The Israelites express no remorse over their own many deaths or those of the tribe of Benjamin, or their decision to murder every Benjamite, including every Benjamite woman and child. Remarkably and inexplicably, their only concern after the butchery was that the six hundred Benjamite men who had escaped

---

1. 17:8, 18:1, 19:1, and 21:25.
2. See chapters 10–12.

the slaughter had no women with whom to breed children and this would result in the extinction of one of the twelve Israelite tribes.[3] This concern seemed unresolvable since they had taken an oath not to give any of their daughters to Benjamite men.[4]

No thought is given to allowing the Benjamites to solve their own problem or to encouraging them to marry Canaanite women. Instead they devised a nefarious and unrestrained plan that involved still another civil war (the third in the book), multiple rapes, and an almost childish maneuver to override their oath.[5]

The Israelites investigated and discovered that there was only one Israelite city, Jabesh-gilead in Transjordan,[6] that did not send any of its citizens to serve in the Israelite force against Benjamin.[7] They recalled that they had sworn "he

---

3. Kaufmann notes that the chapter gives no reason why the Israelites murdered the Benjamite women and children – nonvirgins and virgins – and those of Jabesh-gilead, except for four hundred virgins. He surmises that the only reason they did not kill the four hundred was because they wanted virgins for the surviving Benjamites. However, there is a close parallel to this incident. In Numbers 31:17–18, the Israelites were told to kill all the captured Midianites except for the virgins because the Midianites seduced the Israelites to worship idols by using female seductive powers. It seems that in Numbers 31, the virgins were spared because they were not involved in the seduction. No reason is given why the male children were killed.

4. I describe in detail in chapter 12 why the ancients believed that they could not annul a vow. We can suppose that the Israelites took their oath in the heat of battle and that they would not have done so when coolheaded. This made no difference; once the vow was made, it could not be annulled.

5. Readers who suppose that God was involved in every occurrence in the book of Judges and who also suppose that the Israelites' seeking out God's will should be taken literally and not as internal human deliberations have difficulty trying to explain why God was not involved in the decision to engage in a third civil war that would end in the Israelites killing innocent people and violating their vow. Furthermore, the chapter states explicitly that the Israelites made the decision after deliberation. If they truly always sought divine guidance for other wars, why didn't they do so here?

6. From this time on, the city of Jabesh-gilead felt attached to Benjamin. Later, when King Saul of the tribe of Benjamin was killed and his and his son's body were hung by the pagan forces to humiliate them, some people of Jabesh-gilead heroically rescued their bodies and gave them a proper burial. See I Samuel 11 and 31, and II Samuel 2 and 21:12.

7. This episode is very difficult. First, it is hard to believe that this was the only Israelite town whose citizens hadn't joined the military force. Second, why should the entire town be guilty for the failure of eligible men to enlist? Third, why were women and children killed? Fourth, how did the Israelites determine that a girl was a virgin? (Rashi and Radak quote the Talmud that offers the rather strange idea that the women were placed over barrels of wine. Nonvirgins turned the wine sour, but virgins did not affect the wine.)

[who does not join the military force] shall be killed." They marched in a civil war against this town, killed every inhabitant, including women and children, and saved only virgins to give to the Benjamites.

But they found only four hundred virgins in Jabesh-gilead. They gave the four hundred virgins to four hundred Benjamites and told the remaining two hundred Benjamite survivors that the city of Shiloh celebrated a holiday in which girls would go out to the field and dance.[8] They gave the two hundred Benjamites directions to the city, suggested that they hide just beyond the field, and when sufficient girls gather, they should rush out and snatch a girl and take her home as a wife.[9]

### EHRLICH INTERPRETATIONS AND MY COMMENTS

1. Ehrlich points out the ridiculous belief of the Israelites that they are not violating their oath. They gave Benjamites four hundred Israelite virgins from Jabesh-gilead – this was a clear break. While they did not "directly" hand over two hundred Israelite women from Shiloh to the Benjamites, they told them how to abduct the women and even gave them directions to the city. Similarly, the Israelites breached their oath when they swore to the Gibeonites that they would treat them peacefully, by forcing them to be hewers of wood and drawers of water.[10] Ehrlich adds that since the author of this chapter thought the Israelites could ignore their oath with

---

8. The chapter does not reveal if only the inhabitants of Shiloh observed the holiday in this manner, and what holiday was it. Some, such as Radak, say it was Yom Hakipurim or Av 15. The Babylonian Talmud, *Taanit* 26b and 30b, states there were such dances on these days. It states: "There never were in Israel greater days of joy than the fifteenth of [the month of] Av and the Day of Atonement." Abarbanel thought it was Succoth. Others say it was a pagan feast and still others a holiday celebrating the end of the harvest. Elitzur writes that it is possible that the celebration of Av 15 was a development of the Shiloh celebration, and he informs readers that dancing was a customary celebratory practice in ancient Israel (see Exodus 15:20–21 and 1 Samuel 18:6).

9. This was rape. It is similar to the legend of the Rape of the Sabine Women – traditionally dated as 750 BCE when the first Romans snatched women from Sabine families. The Latin *raptio*, translated "rape," actually means "abduction," and ancients such as Livy tried to mitigate the situation by saying the Romans gained the women's consent after the abduction, but this is unlikely. The story is also similar to the Greek tale about the Messenians who snatched virgins during the feast of Artemis.

10. See my book *Joshua*, Unusual Bible Interpretations chapter 9.

a childlike subterfuge when it is clear that in the early days the Israelites believed they could not do so, this chapter and the one about the Gibeonites may have composed at a later date when the sacredness and unviability of vows changed.

2. I ask: Why weren't the women restricted by the vow? How could they be married to the Benjamites? Should we understand that women were not included in the Israelite oath that they not marry Benjamites because they were women and were excluded from the assembly? Abarbanel thought that women were included in the oath. He wrote that it is clear that the Israelites violated their oath: the women were also included as being forbidden to the Benjamites just as the Israelites considered all Benjamites – including women, children, and virgins – guilty for refusing to give up the rogues who raped the concubine.

3. I also ask: The Babylonian Talmud, *Taanit* 30a, states that the Israelites found a way to avoid their oath – they allowed their children to marry Benjamites. They argued that they had forbid "no man among us, and not our children." Isn't this sophistry, just another childlike evasion?

4. Ehrlich emphasizes that the book of Judges means what it says and Radak is incorrect when he states that there was only one Israelite sanctuary in Canaan; there were many sanctuaries in ancient Israel. Ehrlich also wrote that when the book speaks about a sanctuary in Beth-el it means Shiloh.

5. Proof for Ehrlich's contention is the fact that the Israelites had to give the Benjamites directions for how to get to Shiloh. This indicates that Shiloh was not the only sanctuary in ancient Israel; the Benjamites did not worship there because they had their own sanctuary.

6. Verse 4 states that the Israelites built an altar in Beth-el and offered sacrifices there. Ehrlich writes that in addition to building altars for sacrifices, the ancient Israelites also built nonsacrificial altars as signs of their affection and service to God, as Abraham did in Genesis 12:7. Ehrlich understands that the Israelites built a new altar in Beth-el as a gesture of homage to God, and brought their sacrifices on the altar that was already being used for some time in Beth-el. For, as stated in 20:27, Beth-el had an ark and a priest.[11]

---

11. While tradition states that there was only a single sanctuary at that time and it was in Shiloh, Kaufmann notes that Shiloh only became an important area at the end of the period of the judges.

IRONY

We saw many examples of irony in Judges. Readers who are familiar with 1 Samuel 10 – which narrates events following the era of judges – will recall that the first king of the united Israel was Saul of the tribe of Benjamin who was crowned in Mizpah, the assembly area where the Israelites decided to eradicate this tribe.

# Afterword

Most people suppose that the book of Judges is filled with tales of pious leaders called judges, who performed acts that protected the Israelites and helped form them into a praiseworthy nation. A close reading of the book shows that the early history of Israel was just the opposite.

1. The book reveals that after Joshua's death the Israelites repeatedly worshipped idols; God was angered each time they did so and dispatched pagan nations to harass and kill them. It was only after the people wept and repented that God sent someone to deliver them. The Israelites apparently acted properly as long as these saviors, called judges, lived, but as soon as they died the Israelites lapsed and worshipped idols again.

2. While the tribes were united under Moses and Joshua, during the period of the judges each tribe lived alone and usually acted alone, rarely joining other tribes to aid them against pagan invaders.

3. This was a time "when there was no king in Israel; each man did what he felt was right." As a result there were three civil wars: against Ephraim, Benjamin, and Jabesh-gilead. There were episodes of theft, as when Micah stole money from his mother and money promised to a sanctuary, and when the tribe of Dan took Micah's property, kidnapped his priest, destroyed a peaceful city so they could occupy it, and ironically established a holy sanctuary there. Rapes occurred, such as the rape of the Levite's concubine and the rape of six hundred women that the Israelites gave to the Benjamites males who had escaped the civil war waged against them.

4. While the English translation of the Hebrew *shophtim* is judges, scholars understand the term to denote a governmental and leadership function, not just judicial. Some scholars call these *shophtim* "charismatic leaders."

5. We have no idea how many judges existed. Fourteen[1] or fifteen judges, who

---

1. There were only fourteen judges if Shamgar was a non-Israelite, as discussed in chapter 3, and only thirteen if we delete Samson.

came from many different walks of life, including one woman Deborah, are mentioned in Judges. Two of them, Eli and Samuel, are not mentioned in Judges but in I Samuel. Some of the judges have extended descriptions of their exploits, but little information is given about five judges.

6. The book does not say that three of the judges – Shamgar, Gideon, and Abimelech – served as judges. It also does not say that eight of the judges "saved" Israel – Gideon, Abimelech, Jair, Ibzan, Elon, Abdon, Samson, and Eli.

7. The position of judges never became a fixed part of Israelite society, presumably because it was not an effective form of government.

8. The book seems to extol the tribe of Judah and belittle the tribes of Ephraim and Benjamin. This led some scholars to believe that Judges was composed in the southern kingdom of Judea after the defeat of the northern kingdom of Israel in 722 BCE, in order to humiliate Israel which had seceded from the Judean nation of King David's successor around 922 BCE.

9. Contrary to what many think, there are many obscure passages in Judges, leaving to readers the task to decide how they want to interpret events. There are also many errors in the text, some of them noted on the pages by the Masoretes.

# References

Aeschylus, *Agamemnon*

Altschuler, David, Metzudot David

"Ancient seal may add substance to the legend of Samson," *Science Daily*, August 13, 2012

Babylonian Talmud: *Bava Batra, Berakhot, Gittin, Kiddushin, Megilla, Nazir, Pesachim, Rosh Hashana, Sanhedrin, Shabbat, Shavuot, Sota, Taanit, Yevamot, Yoma*

Berman, Joshua, "Medieval Monasticism and the Evolution of Jewish Interpretation to the Story of Jephthah's Daughter," *Jewish Quarterly Review* 95, no. 2 (2005): 228–256

Boling, Robert G., and G. Ernest Wright, *Judges: Introduction, Translation and Commentary*, Anchor Bible (Garden City: Doubleday, 1982)

Bright, John, *A History of Israel*, 2nd ed. (London: SCM Press, 1972)

Cohen, A., *Joshua and Judges*, The Soncino Books of the Bible (London: Soncino, 1970)

Drazin, Israel, *Joshua*, Unusual Bible Interpretations (Jerusalem: Gefen Publishing House, 2014)

———, *Maimonides and the Biblical Prophets* (Jerusalem: Gefen Publishing House, 2009)

———, *Mysteries of Judaism* (Jerusalem: Gefen Publishing House 2014)

———, *A Rational Approach to Judaism and Torah Commentary* (Jerusalem: Urim, 2007)

Elitzur, Yehuda, *Sefer Shophtim*, Daat Mikra (Jerusalem: Mossad Harav Kook, 1976)

Euripides, *Iphigenia in Tauris*

Gersonides, *The Wars of the Lord*

Ginian, Ilan, *Sefer Shoftim*, The Navi Journey (Jerusalem: Kol Meheichal, 2010)

Ginzberg, Louis, *The Legends of the Jews*, 7 vols. (Philadelphia: Jewish Publication Society, 1901–1938)

Goldstein, Rebecca Newberger, *Plato at the Googleplex: Why Philosophy Won't Go Away* (New York: Pantheon, 2014)

Haran, Menachem, ed., *Shophtim, Olam Hatanakh* (Jerusalem / Tel Aviv: Davidson-Atai, 1995, Hebrew)

Hobbes, Thomas, *The Leviathan* (1651)

*The Holy Scriptures* (Philadelphia: Jewish Publication Society, 1960)

Homer, *The Iliad*

The Interpreter's Bible, vol. 2 (New York/Nashville: Abingdon Press, 1953)

Jacobovici, Simcha, *The Exodus Decoded*, documentary film, directed by James Cameron (2006)

Jerusalem Talmud: *Megilla, Pesachim, Sheviit, Sota*

King, L.W., trans., *The Code of Hammurabi* (CreateSpace, 2014)

Maimonides, Moses, *Guide of the Perplexed*, ed. M. Friedlander (New York: Dover, 1956)

————, *Mishneh Torah*

Martin, J.D., *The Book of Judges*, Cambridge Bible Commentary Series (London: Cambridge University, 1962)

Midrashim: *Genesis Rabba, Leviticus Rabba, Numbers Rabba, Psalms, Seder Olam, Sefer Hayashar, Sifrei, Tanchuma*

Mishnayot: *Nedarim, Sanhedrin, Sota*

Moore, George Foot, *Judges*, International Critical Commentary, 2nd rev. ed. (Edinburgh: T. and T. Clark, 2000)

Pruzansky, Steven, *Judges for Our Time: Contemporary Lessons from the Book of Shoftim* (Jerusalem: Gefen Publishing House, 2009)

Schimmelpfennig, Roland, *Idomeneus*, trans. David Tushingham (London: Oberon, 2014)

Scriptural sources: Amos, I and II Chronicles, Daniel, Ezekiel, Ezra, Hosea, Isaiah, Jeremiah, Job, Joshua, Judges, I and II Kings, Nehemiah, Pentateuch, Psalms, Ruth, I and II Samuel, Septuagint, Zechariah

Soggin, J. Alberto, *Judges*, Old Testament Library (Westminster: John Knox Press, 1981)

Targum Jonathan

# Index

# About the Author

## *Dr. Israel Drazin*

EDUCATION: Dr. Drazin, born in 1935, received three rabbinical degrees in 1957, a BA in theology in 1957, an MEd in psychology in 1966, a JD in law in 1974, an MA in Hebrew literature in 1978, and a PhD with honors in Aramaic literature in 1981. Thereafter, he completed two years of postgraduate study in both philosophy and mysticism and graduated the US Army's Command and General Staff College and its War College for generals in 1985.

MILITARY: Brigadier General Drazin entered army active duty at age twenty-one, as the youngest US chaplain ever to serve on active duty. He served on active duty from 1957 to 1960 in Louisiana and Germany, and then joined the active reserves and soldiered, in increasing grades, with half a dozen units. From 1978 until 1981, he lectured at the US Army Chaplains School on legal subjects. In March 1981, the army requested that he take leave from civil service and return to active duty to handle special constitutional issues. He was responsible for preparing the defense in the trial challenging the constitutionality of the army chaplaincy; the military chaplaincies of all the uniformed services, active and reserve, as well as the Veteran's Administration, were attacked utilizing a constitutional rationale and could have been disbanded. The government won the action in 1984, and Drazin was awarded the prestigious Legion of Merit. Drazin returned to civilian life and the active reserves in 1984 as assistant chief of chaplains, the highest re-serve officer position available in the army chaplaincy, with the rank of brigadier general. He was the first Jewish person to serve in this capacity in the US Army. During his military career, he revolutionized the role of military chaplains, making them officers responsible for the free exercise rights of all military personnel and requiring them to provide for the needs of people of all faiths as well as atheists.

General Drazin completed this four-year tour of duty with honors in March 1988, culminating a total of thirty-one years of military duty.

ATTORNEY: Israel Drazin graduated from law school in 1974 and immediately began a private practice. He handled virtually all manners of suits, including domestic, criminal, bankruptcy, accident, and contract cases. He joined with his son in 1993 and formed offices in Columbia and Dundalk, Maryland. Dr. Drazin stopped actively practicing law in 1997, after twenty-three years, and became "Of Counsel" to the law offices of Drazin and Drazin, PA.

CIVIL SERVICE: Israel Drazin joined the US Civil Service in 1962 and remained a civil service employee, with occasional leave for military duty, until retirement in 1990. At retirement he had accumulated thirty-one years of creditable service. During his US Civil Service career, he held many positions including being an equal opportunity consultant in the 1960s (advising insurance company top executives regarding civil rights and equal employment) and the head of Medicare's Civil Litigation Staff (supervising a team of lawyers who handled suits filed by and against the government's Medicare program). He also served as the director for all Maryland's federal agencies' relationships with the United Fund.

RABBI: Dr. Drazin was ordained as a rabbi in 1957 at Ner Israel Rabbinical College in Baltimore, Maryland, and subsequently received *semichot* from two other rabbis. He entered army active duty in 1957. He left active duty in 1960 and officiated as a weekend rabbi at several synagogues, including being the first rabbi in Columbia, Maryland. He continued the uninterrupted weekend rabbinical practice until 1974 and then officiated as a rabbi on an intermittent basis until 1987. His rabbinical career totaled thirty years.

PHILANTHROPY: Dr. Drazin served as the executive director of the Jim Joseph Foundation, a charitable foundation that gives money to support Jewish education, for just over four years, from September 2000 to November 2004.

AUTHOR: Israel Drazin is the author of twenty-nine books, more than two hundred popular and scholarly articles, and over twenty-seven hundred book and movie reviews. In addition to editing a book on legends, he has written a book about the case he handled for the US Army, children's books, and numerous scholarly books on the philosopher Maimonides and on the Aramaic translation of the Bible. His website is www.booksnthoughts.com.

MEMBERSHIPS AND AWARDS: Brigadier General Drazin is admitted to practice law in Maryland, the Federal Court, and before the US Supreme Court. He is a member of several attorney bar associations and the Rabbinical Council of America (RCA). He was honored with a number of military awards, the RCA 1985 Joseph Hoenig Memorial Award, and the Jewish Welfare Board 1986 Distinguished Service Award. Mayor Kurt Schmoke, of Baltimore, Maryland, named February 8, 1988 "Israel Drazin Day." A leading Baltimore Synagogue named him "Man of the Year" in 1990. He is included in recent editions of *Who's Who in World Jewry*, *Who's Who in American Law*, *Who's Who in Biblical Studies and Archaeology*, and other *Who's Who* volumes.